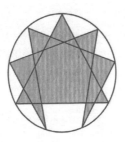

WHAT'S YOUR TRIBE?

An Enneagram guide to human types
at work and play

"Lee Kingma writes about the Enneagram from her perspectives of being a South African, a business executive, and a searcher of life lessons. She guides readers to understanding themselves and others, emphasizing our potential for living together with more kindness, forgiveness, and appreciation. Her writing style is clear, engaging, and accessible to both newcomers and seasoned Enneagram students who wish to build on their knowledge of this rich personality typology. We warmly recommend *What's your Tribe?*"

DON RISO AND RUSS HUDSON, BEST-SELLING AUTHORS OF
PERSONALITY TYPES AND THE WISDOM OF THE ENNEAGRAM
FOR MORE INFORMATION SEE WWW.ENNEAGRAMINSTITUTE.COM

"With this book, Lee Kingma makes a significant contribution to the literature on the Enneagram. *What's Your Tribe?* moves beyond the short sighted self-examination for which the Enneagram is often used and into the realm of how personality style influences our interactions. In the spirit of *Ubuntu*, the author demonstrates how to use the Enneagram as a tool for clarity as we go about shaping each other. This book is a welcome and much-needed reminder that in this complex, global, and sometimes dangerous world we inhabit, we are all members of numerous tribes embedded within other tribes and, ultimately, linked to one large tribe."

MARIO SIKORA, CO-AUTHOR,
AWARENESS TO ACTION: THE ENNEAGRAM, EMOTIONAL INTELLIGENCE, AND CHANGE

"A clear, intelligent introduction to the Enneagram system of personality styles. Short, substantial and 'African flavoured', *What's Your Tribe?* offers many real-life examples plus a test to help readers identify their own personality style. Readers will also discover many actionable ways to apply the Enneagram's insights at work and at home. The book concludes with wise advice on how to use the system both profitably and respectfully. A winner, highly recommended."

THOMAS CONDON, ENNEAGRAM TEACHER, AUTHOR,
THE ENNEAGRAM MOVIE AND VIDEO GUIDE

WHAT'S YOUR TRIBE?

An Enneagram guide to human types
at work and play

LEE KINGMA

DOUBLE
STOREY

What's Your Tribe? An Enneagram guide to human types at work and play
First published 2010
Reprinted April 2010

Juta and Company Ltd
First floor
Sunclare Building
21 Dreyer Street
Claremont
7708

© 2010 Juta & Company Ltd

ISBN: 978-1-77013-079-1

Project Manager: Marlinee Chetty
Editor: Wendy Priilaid
Proofreader: Ethné Clarke
Typesetter: Pete Bosman
Cover designer: Lauren Schofield
Print management by Print Communications

ACKNOWLEDGEMENTS

My deep appreciation goes to my colleagues at Juta for allowing me to treat them as a fishbowl of learning, most especially Rory Wilson, Ishmet Davidson, Lynne du Toit, Sakkie de Villiers, André van Niekerk, Leela Moodley, Wayne Staples, Kirsty Edwards, Tamsyn Jardine, Leigh-Anne Hunter, Lesley Miller, Reetesh Ranchod, Joanita Theron, and Glenda Younge.

Thank you also to the publishing team at Juta for believing in this little tome and for their superb professional support: Sandy Shepherd, Duncan Johansen, Marlinee Chetty, Madelein Meiring, Charles Mackriel and Natasha Talliard.

I wish to acknowledge my prime teachers Don Riso and Russ Hudson for being the routes of my learning of the Enneagram and their works as the chief source of the material and interpretations of this book. I have attempted to acknowledge them and other teachers and authors, but where I have slipped up please know that is has not been intentional. Knowledge is often absorbed subliminally and we do not always remember the exact source.

I am also thankful to Craig O' Flaherty, Charlotte and Allan Peterson and André Slabbert for their generous sharing of wisdom and support of my personal quest.

I thank my coaching and Enneagram community for the learning and fun: Karen White, Roland Cox, Barry Coltham, Anthony Youds, Therese Tomes, Karin MacKenzie, Penny Day and Cathy Clerk.

My appreciation goes to my dear friends for their moral support: Rod and Ina Cronwright, Bryna Zassman, Mike and Sue Davis, and Penny Haw.

Lastly, but most fundamentally, thank you to my family: my much respected and adored husband Ronald, and my precious children Lauren, Hugh, Kirsten and Aiden.

And a bone to my pug, Panda, for his unconditional love.

Rie Kingma

To my darling Cuz

This book is dedicated to you for always being able to predict the weather, and then knowing just how best I need to be held. For being the best chef and win connoisseur, a master builder of our Beehive, a diligent breakfast-in-bed provide and a wise and fun father, and for planning the most adventurous holidays.

CONTENTS

FOREWORD

The Enneagram has an ancient history and tradition as a way of understanding our 'way of being' as humans and the effect we have on the world around us. Much has been written about this way of understanding human behaviour and the choices we make. Too often, though, this descends into descriptions and comparisons that leave readers more confused than when they started.

Lee Kingma's book has a way of making what can sometimes be esoteric and confounding very accessible. Her exploration of the various types of the Enneagram is populated with personal examples and real-life situations in a way which makes the concepts being discussed come to life and understandable. Her slant on the Enneagram types as a series of 'tribes' that we belong to is a metaphor that keeps alive our curiosity to look for similarities that we can relate to and consequences of operating from the perspectives of these types. She concludes with practical choices and possibilities that we can look to from being anchored in a particular type or tribe. She collects a series of perspectives from other authors about the Enneagram types and tabulates these in a way which allows for comparison and integration.

Her specific slant on the Enneagram and its perspective on conflict gives a sense of how conflict arises and its effects, and how different types are able to solve it in unique and particular ways. She also examines change through the perspective of the Enneagram, and the choices and practices that flow from this. Her work is therefore a wonderful source of reference for practitioners such as coaches, leaders and change agents, and anyone looking to develop themselves and others.

Enjoy the journey!

Craig O'Flaherty
director – Centre for Coaching
Graduate School of Business
University of Cape Town

Finding your tribe

ie Enneagram as a guide to human connection at work and play

ɔu, DEAR READER, most likely dipped into this book because you are curious out what really drives your own and others' behaviour. Most of us would some way like to improve our relationships with others and ultimately th ourselves. Moving from World 1.9 to World 2.0 we are challenged with nstant change, information overload, rapid technological advancement, reats to our environment, material greed or the obsessions with our physical pearance. I don't believe that life is necessarily more difficult than it was for r grandparents, but the rate of change is far more rapid, and it is coping with e change that creates so much stress for people.

Often we feel misunderstood, anxious and overwhelmed by life. We set out t to judge others, but we often find that we are either instantly attracted or ɔelled by others. Sometimes relationships start off well and then deteriorate, ving us feeling empty and disappointed.

A universal question that man (and woman!) has faced throughout the ages *Who am I?* I believe that the extent to which we can answer this truthfully ourselves is a huge step in achieving happiness in our lifetime. The other estion is *Why am I here?* This is an even more difficult question and I will not empt to grapple with such a deep philosophical conundrum in this book. wever, it is very likely that when we can answer the first question with some th, this will bring clarity in finding some interesting possibilities for the ɔnd one.

I accept that there are many ways for us to approach these deep questions. beaming light for me in getting some very useful answers to the first estion *Who am I?* has been through studying a personality typology called Enneagram. It has been a gift to make sense of the people around me and, re importantly, made me aware of how I affect others in how I behave in my ly life.

Searchers of the truth

When you browse in the self-help section of your favourite bookshop you w
notice a wide range of books on offer. Some appear superficial and trite but the
are intriguing gems that do offer practical insights in living our lives with mo
meaning. Those are the ones that are likely to be on your personal bookshelf.

What I find more intriguing is that this section even exists in bookshops ar
that so many people can be found browsing there. Publishers tell us that sel
help is a very lucrative subject area. It has grown due to people taking an intere
in and responsibility for their own psychological and spiritual developmer
Some may feel cynical about the role of religion in our modern lives and wh
they were taught by parents and teachers. Others are just curious to see wh
new development and thinking is out there in the knowledge world.

There are those teachers who are critical of people dipping into o
philosophy after another, i.e. skipping from numerology to astrology to t
Eastern religions. I see no harm in this as it demonstrates that people are ke
to explore until they find the models or philosophies that make sense and gi
meaning to their existence. Even those who have found a meaningful bel
system may still keep looking because they have an open mind and are curio
to see what is new or a rediscovered truth.

I see this trend as an encouraging sign that people are intrigued about w
they are and want to be more awake to living energetically.

So, why have I written this book, and what do I hope to add to peop
understanding of self and others?

A model for understanding our behaviour

It is my intention to share what I know about this model called the Enneagra
In providing you with some basic knowledge of the Enneagram I hope to g
you greater awareness of your motivations for certain habitual responses
situations and provide you with alternatives for more constructive ones. T
model defines nine dominant personality types. Each has its blind spots,
fixations, and gifts. The gifts are beacons that can guide people in their quest
self-development and personal growth. The blind spots or fixations are aspe
of behaviour that create conflict or in some way prevent people from reach
their full potential.

My personal experience

I have always been curious about people's behaviour and what motivates them. This curiosity was probably the main trigger to finding my work expression in the field of human resources and continuing lifelong studies in the field of personality typology. Early on in my career I observed a clear link in how people's motivation and emotional intelligence (EQ) equate to their performance and ultimately to a business's financial results.

In my personal life I noticed how people who are happy and live constructive lives are more self-aware than those who just keep making the same behavioural mistakes as if they are on autopilot or asleep.

As I reached midlife I began to observe the 'successful malcontents'. I noticed people who were relatively successful in their careers and material lives but who still seemed unhappy, often unkind and critical about others and just generally unaware of how their spurts of bad behaviour affected those around them.

In my work life I had been exposed to a number of personality typology models and psychometric tests which were used mostly for recruitment purposes. My master's thesis was based on analysing a psychometric test which purported to measure honesty in recruiting security staff. My conclusion was that this test was not reliable or accurate and should therefore not be used in the company where I was working at the time. Needless to say I left this company soon afterwards.

My career move was a bit like life handing me a bouquet in that I landed a position as the group human resources manager for a medium-sized, well-established and progressive publishing company. My new manager was impressive in his intellectual capacity but I soon realised that unless I got to understand him really well, I would not be able to work with him.

During meetings he was often dismissive towards others and had outbursts of anger towards people when he disagreed with them on certain issues. This anger was once directed at me in a meeting when I was giving cautious advice regarding a critical industrial relations situation. This altercation left me feeling demeaned and worthless.

I had previously attended an introduction course to the Enneagram, and I read Riso and Hudson's *The Wisdom of the Enneagram*. After the above-mentioned experience I felt intuitively guided back to this book. The description of the Type Eight *Challenger** was very accurate and insightful in describing the behaviour traits of my new CEO boss. At the same time I saw my young son portrayed in examples of this behaviour.

I have used Riso-Hudson Type Names throughout. Copyright 2009 The Enneagram Institute. All Rights Reserved. Used with Permission.

The knowledge that the apple of my eye and this difficult new boss we[r]e from the same *tribe* had a profound effect on how I have viewed people sin[ce] this realisation. I finally absolutely got it that I could not change either of ther[m] but instead that I could choose to react differently to their behaviour. I beca[me] more firm with both my boss and my son in standing my ground, yet alwa[ys] being respectful towards them. Understanding the fire that comes from the[ir] gut in how they often overreact to situations made me feel both more powerf[ul] and yet compassionate when they lost their cool.

This manager became a mentor and supporter in my thirst for knowi[ng] more about the Enneagram and using it as a tool for practical understandi[ng] of human beings in the workplace. I was privileged to participate in all of t[he] Riso and Hudson Enneagram training interventions. Attending a course in t[he] scenic Welsh farmlands and then the magnificent forestlands of Stroudsbu[rg] in the US also created wonderful travel opportunities. I met wonderful peop[le] from many different countries who made enormous sacrifices, driven by th[e] curiosity of gaining a deeper understanding of human beings.

My executive team noticed the benefits of this knowledge in growing their o[wn] leadership skills and their team effectiveness. They valued the connection betwe[en] well-functioning teams and good business results. After the *Challenger* mana[ger] left, I reported to a wise Type One *Reformer* for a brief period before he left to ta[ke] on a more challenging opportunity. He encouraged me to attend the Europe[an] Enneagram conference in the mystical and spiritual village of Assisi in Italy.

My current manager is a lively Type Seven *Enthusiast* who has worked [in] global companies in both London and Paris. She also saw the benefit of [the] Enneagram model, which she put to the test with her pragmatic busin[ess] experience and knowledge. She encouraged and sponsored me to complet[e a] doctoral thesis on Utilising the Enneagram in Dealing with Workplace Confl[ict]. Recently I presented a paper on my thesis in calm Denmark, a land drape[d in] autumn colours during the time of my visit where I was also able to appreci[ate] its ancient history.

In my personal life the knowledge and application to the Enneagram [has] been truly transforming. It has been a great big AHA! to see myself more clea[rly]. Admittedly, at times it has been quite painful to admit to my fixations, but [it] lessens with the knowledge that the Enneagram can help me to find a wa[y to] show up hopefully as a more integrated human being. The stupid mistakes [and] decisions I made as a younger person now have a context and I could finall[y let] go of past guilt and consequent hurt caused to myself and others.

Finally I could also forgive my parents for my chaotic childhood in truly eing that they made their life decisions based on who they were and what they new at the time.

In my family, the members identify with the following Enneagram types:

My father, as the Type Six *Loyalist*, experienced enormous anxiety as a young ild and this led to his challenges with alcohol throughout his life. My mother, a Type Two *Helper*, was mortally wounded when my father left her for another oman and has spent her life learning to forgive.

As a mother I appreciate my eldest daughter's Type Four *Individualist's* creative ays instead of wanting her to fit into society and its norms. My son-in-law, a pe Nine *Peacemaker*, shies away from any family dissent and needs time out : long cycle rides, which typify the zoning-out tendency of the *Peacemaker*. younger daughter, a Type Three *Achiever*, is often reminded that my love her is not conditional on her next competitive achievement. And my young pe Eight *Challenger* son I hold with firm love when he shows his very direct ger when things do not go his way.

Already blessed with an amazing husband, I fell in love with him much more ply. In the past I was often irritated by his factual contradiction of my views. ow understand that he needs to evaluate concepts from all angles and that contradiction is in no way directed at me personally, but rather is his way of king sense of various factual options. This is typical behaviour of the Type e *Investigator*.

am no longer as irritated by others' foibles and perceived hurts and ction of me or my opinions. I love my friends more unconditionally, and relationships at work have more clarity and empathy. Even my pug dog ys my company more!

m because we are'

know that as human beings we were created to fit into a socialised ironment – the extent to which we battle with this is often our pathology. happiness is usually impacted on to the extent that we interact well within families, circle of friends, places of learning or work teams. In South Africa efer to this interpersonal interaction as *ubuntu*, meaning 'I am because we This means that a person is a person through others, and through his or her ionship with, and recognition by, other people. *Ubuntu* emphasises human rdependence and the relationships between people.

Genuine corporate social investment – not the kind which is intended to make scorecards look good – also demonstrates *ubuntu* when businesses reach out to previously disadvantaged communities to offer skills and resources which ultimately bring about true transformation for all rather than enrichment for few where the sole criterion is race.

Ubuntu is the basis of African philosophy and holds dear the principle of selflessness, of not being obsessed with material wealth and of having the capacity of forgiveness. In many ways it is the opposite of the American dream of material wealth and competition.

The peaceful political transition in South Africa from a totalitarian state to a true democracy in 1994 owes itself largely to the spirit of *ubuntu*. The lack of revenge from those who were previously oppressed and the spirit of forgiveness resulted in a transition without bloodshed. The miracle has been that largely as South Africans have been able to discover one another with a new curiosity and respect.

Ubuntu is similar to the Buddhist ideal of compassion. It reflects the commitment of the Buddha and his followers to be concerned about the welfare of all sentient beings. It is also an important Christian principle which is held the notion of doing unto others as you would wish them to do unto you.

It is in this human connection that I yearn for the understanding of the Enneagram in how we as human beings can become more forgiving and skilled in how we relate to one another. I recommend that to live the true spirit of *ubuntu* we need to first figure out who we are or to which Enneagram tribe we belong. Once we have a deeper understanding of our tribe, utilising knowledge of the Enneagram, we will have more self-awareness to show up decent individuals who have sufficient emotional intelligence (EQ) to interact optimally with others.

My purpose in writing this book

I am not a psychologist. This book is not meant to be an academic treatise how to apply the knowledge of the Enneagram in dealing with pathology have written it from the perspective of applying the model to ordinary people – amazing people – all the people whom I have connected with since gaining understanding of the Enneagram as a mother, wife, friend, daughter, sibling and human resources practitioner. I have also not attended to the more spiritual aspects of the Enneagram in this book, as I believe the first hurdle of spiritual discovery is to deal with our personality fixations before embarking on the to enlightenment. However, this can happen simultaneously and I recommend further reading to those who wish to pursue discovering their spirituality through the Enneagram.

Bees, especially the queen bee, have always fascinated me, and I have a small bee tattooed on my left shoulder in honour of the queen bee. I respect bees' order and industriousness. The output of their hard work is steeped in usefulness as they produce the miracle substance of honey, and pollinate nature in the process. If anyone messes with them they can defend themselves decisively with a mean sting. I am mesmerised by their colour, and their buzz is like the chant of perennial monks. A hive of bees illustrates the collective effort of teamwork. Although their tasks are defined in objectives, for example finding an appropriate hive, producing honey or looking after the safety of the queen, the focus remains on the well-being of the colony. The queen bee leads with understated dignity – she is a leader of compassion and structure, and can show her drones the way from danger to alternative opportunities.

I liken writing this book to the path of the queen bee – when she finds the pollen which can produce honey, she has a natural call to create the context for her drones to share. My understanding of the Enneagram is the honey which I need to share and in this way hopefully add more clarity and sweetness to others' lives.

CHAPTER ONE

Knowing yourself

IT IS COMMONLY AGREED that we are defined largely by our personalities. But what do we mean by 'personality'? The term comes from the Latin word *persona*, which means 'mask'. This is interesting as it suggests that our personality is just a cover for who we really are. I believe that the personality can be likened to an artichoke. As we peel away the layers of who we pretend to be, we get to the delicious heart inside – the real gem of our true selves.

A more scientific way to understand personality is to view it as a hypothetical entity seated in the brain, which is the ruling institution of the human organism. In interaction with any situation, it determines all the behaviour of the individual throughout life. The nature of the individual's personality can therefore be deduced from his or her total life history. Personality consists of a dynamic set of needs, fantasies, opinions, hypotheses and expectations which influence the individual's perceptions and interpretations of his or her world which in turn influence his or her behaviour.

Personality is also explained as a composite of factors. Different theories of personality emphasise different factors but, broadly, personality consists of:
- Genetics
- Traits
- Culture/society
- Learning
- Personal choice
- Unconscious mechanisms.

Just to add to the mystery of personality it has also been suggested that every human being is
- like every other human being
- like some other human beings.

Constructivism

Another way to understand why we all behave differently is to understand the concept of constructivism. This means that people create their realities through the meanings they link to what they observe.

The Chilean biologist, Humberto Maturana (2004), uses the illustration of frogs as an analogy to explain constructivism:

> When we see a frog catch a fly, we assume that the fly looks much the same to the frog as it does to us. In fact, however, the frog's eyes allow it to perceive the fly only when it moves, and then just as a vague moving shape. The frog therefore has access to the reality of the world only as it is filtered by its sensory apparatus. In the same way we construct our own reality by the means of the eyes with which we see it, and it is filtered reality.

This is why Maturana says that five members of a family do not have five different views of the same family, but that five different families are actually created, based on the five members' completely different sets of meanings. Similarly, five members of a family would have five very different views, depending on their inherent different Enneagram types. Some members might share a type, but other nuances of Enneagram theory, such as their wings (see Chapter 13), levels of integration and subtypes, would affect the way they view the world. These theories will be covered further on in this book. However, the 'tints' of personality are created by nurturing, i.e. parental, peer and societal influences, which play an important role in the way individuals develop their views and sets of meanings.

Why do we behave badly?

Most of us by the time we are adults have a clear theoretical understanding of how to treat ourselves and others in a compassionate way. Why is it then that we often react badly to situations – as a course of habit? We usually regret our reaction after an incident, but often we will still defend our behaviour. Our intentions most likely were not to harm a relationship, but in the moment we behaved badly.

You may have

lost your temper – roared at others like a lion

not stood your ground – hiding in the shallow waters like a crocodile

been overcritical – stinging others like a bee

been entitled and manipulative – corralling the herd like an elephant

- used someone for your own gain – changed your colours like a chameleon
- become moody and uncooperative – skulked into a corner like a cat
- acted with mental superiority – closed your wise eye like an owl
- distrusted yourself and others unnecessarily – skittered off into the bush like a buck
- let others down because of your selfish agenda – flown off to the next flower like a butterfly.

We all fall into these traps but some we fall into more regularly.

Your disappointment in your reaction is the first step in becoming more self-aware. Each individual has a way of seeing the world. Self-awareness occurs when we are conscious of our inner motivations or reactions. Personal mastery occurs when we are self-aware *and* react in a constructive manner, thus displaying a high degree of emotional intelligence.

Emotional intelligence

Emotional intelligence (EQ) can best be described as an individual's ability to monitor his or her own and others' emotions, to discriminate between the positive and negative effects of emotion and to use emotional information to guide thinking and actions. From a scientific point of view, emotional intelligence is the synthesis of knowing, thinking and feeling. This amalgam can be viewed as a psycho-physiological synchronisation if it includes the effect of the body's physiological responses. The greater the degree of overlap between the knowing, thinking, feeling and responding aspects of awareness, the more positive is the physiological synchronisation. This also corresponds with the Enneagram theory as it relates to the Centres, which are discussed in Chapter 13 (i.e. the thinking awareness relating to the Head Centre, the feeling awareness relating to the Emotional or Feeling Centre, and the knowing awareness relating to the Moving or Instinctive Centre). The Enneagram theory proposes that when these three Centres are aligned, the individual operates at a healthy psychological level.

Intelligence (IQ) test results for teenagers remain constant when compared to IQ tests results done when they are adults, using age-appropriate complexity test batteries. Unlike IQ, which changes little after the teenage years, emotional intelligence (EQ) seems to be largely learned, and it continues to develop as people go through life and learn from their experiences. The good news for adults, therefore, is that they can grow their EQ, even though their IQ remains static.

Self-awareness

When people have the ability to observe their own behaviour, this becomes a major source of self-knowledge. It serves people to have the capability to be 'external' observers of their own behaviour so that they can understand their feelings, attitudes and traits. We grow from impulse, where we simply react to the world, to instinct, where we are ruled by emotions, to intellect, where the mind starts to have some awareness of and influence over our destiny.

Many of us are stuck in unhealthy ways of seeing the world and thus reacting to situations as if we were dragging an enormous bag of old behaviour patterns around all the time. This can be illustrated in the example of a woman who irritated her family circle and often turned other people off. Her habitual behaviour pattern was of seemingly being generous to others by giving them small gifts – usually things which she no longer required. However, once the gift was accepted, there was always the implicit expectation of a favour which was to be returned. This behaviour can be likened to reaching into a bag of old tricks for a familiar way of reacting instead of basing reaction on a fresh, more accurate assessment of the situation. It is like watching old tapes on a screen instead of concentrating on the live action reported by the senses.

People build their identity from their chaotic and unconscious impulses. If people observe themselves carefully, they will discover that what goes on inside, the constant churning of their mechanical responses, like the machinery of the personality grinding along on its own. It is in recognising these responses that the Enneagram can be such an effective tool to help people to observe themselves and thereby get some 'distance' from their personality.

Our egos are usually to blame for us not reaching our full potential. A healthy ego is required to manoeuvre our way through modern life, but an unhealthy ego leads us to being fixated with fear, anger or self-promotion. This unhealthy ego can be viewed as an unconscious blob residing in the basement of development potential. Each of the Enneagram types has strengths, but when controlled by the ego these same strengths become our weaknesses. So, for example, Type Threes are ambitious and concerned with success. However, when this strength is overplayed or becomes a fixation, then Type Threes may become workaholics, lie and cheat to be better than others and neglect their dear ones because they have come in the way of their success.

All Enneagram types are in danger of allowing the ego to control their personality essence or strength, and to turn them into their shadow selves if they are not self-aware. It is in this way that the model becomes a map to show us how to be awake to the paradoxes of our beings.

In the next chapter we will explore the Enneagram with regard to its history theory, validity and application.

CHAPTER TWO

Understanding the Enneagram

THE ENNEAGRAM

Peacemaker

9

Challenger 8   1 Reformer

Enthusiast 7   2 Helper

6   3 Achiever

Loyalist

5   4

Investigator   Individualist

THE WORD *ENNEAGRAM* (pronounced 'ANY-a-gram') is derived from Greek – *ennea* meaning 'nine' and *grammos* meaning 'figure'.

The Enneagram symbol has very ancient roots. Many myths abound regarding its inception, and the history at best can only be more accurately reconstructed from 1900. What is amazing about it is the current application of its veracity in describing human nature. Highly trained and experienced psychologists who work with human frailties daily have found the Enneagram to be accurate in diagnosing clients' dysfunctional behaviours. In our present time we are more aware of how people need guidance and answers in dealing with the challenges of living in mental health if we are to have any taste of our yearnings for happiness.

Today more than ever before, people are aware that they should search for happiness and normalcy as a birthright and that psychological health is not usually achieved accidentally but needs to be an intention which receives our attention if it is to be our manifestation.

The Enneagram is one of the few systems that concerns itself with normal and high-functioning behaviour rather than pathology. It condenses a great deal of psychological wisdom into a compact system that is relatively easy to understand.

A brief history of the Enneagram

George Ivanovich Gurjieff, a Greek-Armenian born in 1875, brought the Enneagram symbol to the modern world. Gurdjieff became interested in esoteric knowledge as a young man and travelled the world with a group of friends to piece together the lost science of human transformation. This group travelled to Egypt, Afghanistan, Greece, Persia, India and Tibet spending time in monasteries and remote sanctuaries. On Gurdjieff's travels, possibly in Afghanistan or Turkey, he came across the Enneagram symbol. Gurdjieff taught a complex study of psychology, spirituality and cosmology in St Petersburg and Moscow, using the Enneagram as a process model, not as a personality typology.

A young Bolivian student, Oscar Ichazo, learned about the Enneagram from Gurdjieff. In the 1950s he discovered the connection between the Enneagram symbol and the personality types. In 1970 a noted psychiatrist, Claudio Naranjo went to study with Ichazo in Italy. Naranjo expanded Ichazo's brief descriptions of the personality types.

Don Riso, then a Jesuit seminarian, learned the basic Enneagram theory from Naranjo. Riso went on to define the nine levels of development in 1977. He also confirmed the psychological correlations of the Enneagram with the works of Jung, Freud and Horney. Today there are many qualified teachers of the Enneagram, many books have been authored, psychologists work with the model in a clinical environment and it is also used in the workplace and at business schools as a leadership model.

Important aspects of the Enneagram theory

People do not change from one basic type to another. Although they do learn new skills and coping mechanisms, the foundation of personality remains the same. The eternal debate regarding personality has often focused on the question whether personality type is due to 'nurture' or 'nature'. An investigation was the

nducted to establish whether the Enneagram theory holds that personality
its are due to genetics or to childhood experiences.

Extensive Enneagram studies carried out at Stanford University discovered
at after only six months, neonates displayed nine distinct ways of relating
d that these exactly matched the nine Enneagram types. This suggests that
rents add 'tints' to personalities through the way they raise their children. The
untry and place where nurturing takes place adds colour and flavour, but the
sic personality governs the way people see the world, confirm their view and
ate their own reality.

The descriptions of personality type are universal and apply equally to males
d females. There is no evidence that any one country has more people of a
tain type than another. This also applies to race, creed and colour. A country
y reflect a certain culture, e.g. the US may be viewed as a Type Three culture
e to its quest for material achievement. Germany may be viewed as a Type One
ture due to the value placed on perfectionism and exact standards. Denmark
y be viewed as a Type Six culture due to the high trust levels and loyalty
vards kin and country. I believe that South Africa veers between Type Eight
d Nine cultures. Both are in the *Instinctive Triad* – Type Eight is indicative
aggression and control, and Type Nine can demonstrate sloth and the need
much participation but a lack in delivery. On the upside, Type Eight also
icates care for the vulnerable and Type Nine is concerned with peace and
lusivity, or *ubuntu*.

People's traits within the personality type may apply to different degrees
individuals and fluctuate among the healthy, average or unhealthy levels,
ending on how they cope with life stresses. Gurdjieff, the 'father' of the
eagram model, further challenges the concept of emotional stability by
gesting that the greatest mistake is to believe that a human being remains a
stant unity. According to Gurdjieff, human beings never stay the same for
ger than a short period. They continually change; they rarely stay constant
n for a single hour.

he Enneagram uses numbers to designate each type, providing an unbiased,
rthand way of indicating much about a person without being pejorative or
icating pathology. There is no ranking value to the numbers, i.e. it is no
er to be a Type Nine than a Type Two.

No type is inherently better or worse than another. We may identify with
characteristics of a number of the types, but we only have one true type, or
e, to which we belong.

Critics of the Enneagram have stated that typing puts one in a box. Howev
it is suggested that most of us are in boxes already due to our habitual ways
reacting to situations as described in the beginning of this chapter. What t
Enneagram gives us is an understanding for our behaviour together with sor
options or choices to change our reactions. As we become more self-awa
i.e. observing our behaviour, we can make changes to the ways we habitua
respond. Although we will recognise personality traits of all the types within
we have one dominant type.

It is important to remain mindful of why we are curious to learn abc
the Enneagram. It should never be because we want to manipulate or juc
others, but rather that we are curious to learn to be more effective in h
we communicate and to treat ourselves and others with more compassi
and tolerance.

Embracing all religions

It is important to note that the Enneagram in no way favours or excludes a
religious belief system. Its historic routes can in some way be connected to
the three prophetic religions. The only belief system that might be opposed
its theory would be one steeped in fundamentalism. It is, however, sugges
that a fundamentalist perspective would have difficulty in objectively review
any alternative way of understanding human behaviour.

A brief descriptions of the nine types

The following are the basic type names of personality for each of the n
personality types. These are all couched in positive terms, and further in
book we will uncover some of the blind spots for each type, which help u
our self-development. The types are often described by different type nai
depending on the author or teacher. I have chosen to use the type names fr
Riso and Hudson (1996), my original teachers.

You will notice that I always start with Type Eight, rather than Type C
This is because Type Eight is the first type in the Centre that deals with
Instinctive Centre. The Centres are explained more fully in Chapter 13.

Type Eight – *the Challenger*

Challengers are assertive, resourceful, strong, straight-talking and at times wi
They can inspire others to buy into their vision and are the natural leaders o
Enneagram. They are shrewd in finding answers to problems and will not ea

defeated. They show their anger easily and may intimidate more reserved
ople. Type Eights have a gentle heart which they typically only show to those
10m they can trust and will stand up for those who are vulnerable.

mous Type Eights
)nald Trump, Golda Meir, Sol Kerzner, Anton Rupert

pe Nine – *the Peacemaker*

acemakers are easygoing, patient, diplomatic and serene. They may at times
ne out on a daydream and are happy to wait for an outcome rather than push
:ir own agenda. They will carefully check out the facts of a situation before
icting. Although they do not show their anger directly, they may at times
: back at those who annoy them in subtle ways. Type Nines can be stubborn
out sticking to their own opinions but will find a non-confrontational way
do this.

mous Type Nines
ieen Elizabeth, Ronald Reagan, Ernie Els, Morné du Plessis

pe One – *the Reformer*

formers are highly disciplined, perfectionistic, opinionated and idealistic.
ey hold strong views on the things which they value and can be quite critical
those who do not agree with their opinions. They can be hard on themselves,
:d they are highly responsible and impatient in taking action on things which
:d to be corrected. Words such as 'should' and 'wrong' and 'right' are prevalent
:heir vocabulary.

nous Type Ones
·ryl Streep, Hillary Clinton, Nelson Mandela, Helen Zille

)e Two – *the Helper*

'pers are caring, warm, thoughtful and generous. They are keen to flatter
.ers with compliments and are openly affectionate – often physically. They
motivated to satisfy others' needs and may in the process neglect themselves.
)e Twos are naturally empathetic and enjoy nurturing and finding ways to
ke people happy.

nous Type Twos
ther Teresa, Bill Cosby, Desmond Tutu, Emily Hobhouse

Type Three – *the Achiever*

Achievers are energetic, competitive, competent and adaptable. They are ofte
ambitious, either for themselves or for those nearest to them. They avoid failu
at all cost. Type Threes are conscious of how others see them and need to ma
a positive impression on others. When they excel they often become role mode
in their communities.

Famous Type Threes

Barack Obama, Oprah Winfrey, Charlize Theron, Jacob Zuma

Type Four – *the Individualist*

Individualists are sensitive, experience their feelings deeply and often percei
themselves as different to others. They usually have some creative outlet a
may at times be moody and introspective. They are highly imaginative a
intuitive. Type Fours can easily be hurt by others and may in turn be passiona
in their responses.

Famous Type Fours

Jackie Onassis, Jeremy Irons, Ingrid Jonker, Nataniël

Type Five – *the Investigator*

Investigators are private, analytical, often preoccupied in their thoughts a
focused on what holds their attention. They are keen to find out how things
together and are motivated to gain deeper knowledge of the things that inter
them. They can see the world without sentiment and enjoy time alone w
hobbies or just mulling in their own thoughts.

Famous Type Fives

Albert Einstein, Bill Gates, Gill Marcus, Mark Shuttleworth

Type Six – *the Loyalist*

Loyalists are reliable, organised, cautious and prepared for the unexpected. T
usually keep friends for life. Type Sixes can spend much energy worrying abo
things that never happen and may see negatives more easily than positi
They may be suspicious of others' motives and find it hard to make decisio
when confronted with choices. Phobic Type Sixes are outwardly fearful and s
approval. Counterphobic Type Sixes confront their fears. Both of these aspe
can appear in the same person.

Famous Type Sixes

Princess Diana, Richard Nixon, Thabo Mbeki, Clem Sunter

Type Seven – *the Enthusiast*

Enthusiasts are impulsive, outgoing and optimistic, and seek adventure and variety in life. They easily respond to stimuli and may be seen to be superior to others in the views they hold. They can overindulge in the pleasures of life and may become scattered. They avoid painful situations and are usually entertaining and fun to be around.

Famous Type Sevens
Richard Branson, Liza Minnelli, Barry Ronge, Marc Lottering

The validity of the Enneagram

Although there are many different teachers, researchers and authors on the Enneagram, they are all in implicit agreement on the nine types and the definitions for the traits although they may use different language to illustrate these as behaviours. It is unfortunate that some students of the Enneagram have become 'precious' about who their teachers are and in some way need to make these teachers into 'gurus'. I believe that this is a futile exercise as what is most relevant and practical to people is usually the true definer of knowledge and wisdom.

For any information to be valued in the world, it has to be 'actionable'. The Enneagram is often used in ways that are limited to typology or the cataloguing of common traits. The ability to see the trait patterns in oneself and others is useful in many ways but the understanding of what inspires these trait patterns is even more useful. The Enneagram should be understood as a system of how we pay attention – this serves or appears to serve to achieve evolutionary success. The nine types are approaches to interacting with the world. For whatever reason, we prefer one way of paying attention and tend to rely on it significantly more than on the others, sometimes to our detriment.

I recently met a lady who spent the first ten minutes after introduction complaining about how as a European she experienced South African standards very low. Shop windows were dirty, the water was cloudy in floral arrangements and she could not enjoy a meal out as the cutlery was not pristinely clean. She went on to mention how her son complains that she is forever teaching others how to get things right. Although a charming person she is clearly not happy as her world is so very imperfect. I would suggest that this tendency to pay attention to what is wrong in the world has little to do with her being of European descent, but rather due to her seeing the world through the lenses of a dissatisfied Type One *Reformer*.

Abnormal behaviour patterns

It is difficult to qualify what we mean by 'normal' behaviour. In fact, sometime true brilliancy or creativity is found in those who do not behave in what socie would consider being normal.

In my work in human resources I have mostly come across the category people who would be considered to be behaving at average levels. Most da we cope well with the challenges that come our way, and sometimes we ev show signs of being truly enlightened, wise and compassionate. And then the are those times when people lose it and might be classified as showing signs abnormal behaviour.

When this is constant, people are not likely to cope in the workplace a would most likely be incapacitated and should be treated by either psychologi or psychiatrists. Systems of classifications of abnormal behaviour date back ancient times. The 19th-century German psychiatrist Emil Kraepelin (1913) generally considered to be the first modern theorist to develop a comprehensiv model of classification based on the distinctive features, or 'symptoms' associat with abnormal behaviour patterns. The most commonly used classificati system today is largely a development and extension of Kraepelin's work: *Diagnostic and Statistical Manual of Mental Disorders (DSM)*, published by American Psychiatric Association (2003).

The latest version of the *DSM*, published in 2000, is the *DSM-IV-TR* of fourth edition (*DSM-IV*). Research is currently taking place to publish the fi edition, which is projected to take place in 2012.

It is interesting to note that of the ten personality disorders that have b identified in the *DSM-IV* Axis II, all can be linked to abnormal behaviour in unhealthy or dysfunctional aspects of each the nine Enneagram types. Two these can be linked to the Type Five, the *Investigator*. The abnormal behavi associated with Type Seven is classified under mood disorders. It is not sugges that the personality disorders listed here are solely linked to one Enneagr type.

Following are the Enneagram types with the associated persona disorder:

Type Eight, the *Challenger* – antisocial personality disorder
Type Nine, the *Peacemaker* – dependent personality disorder
Type One, the *Reformer* – obsessive-compulsive personality disorder
Type Two, the *Helper* – histrionic personality disorder
Type Three, the *Achiever* – narcissistic personality disorder

Type Four, the *Individualist* – avoidant personality disorder
Type Five, the *Investigator* – schizoid and schizotypal disorders
Type Six, the *Loyalist* – paranoid personality disorder
Type Seven, the *Enthusiast* – bipolar disorders

is important to note that we should not try to be self-appointed psychiatrists
d label people as such, as these conditions would only manifest in extreme
es and should be diagnosed by qualified clinicians.

In the chapters dealing with each type, I will give a brief description of these
orders – and a description of the highest behaviour which every type can
ive to becoming a truly Awakened Being.

e Enneagram in Business

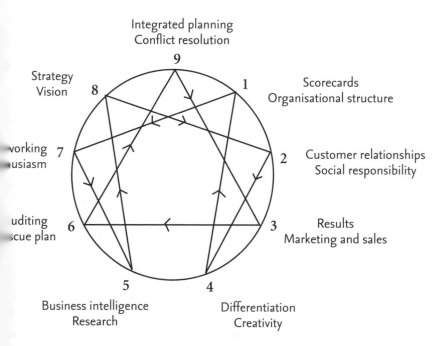

SYSTEMS ENNEAGRAM

Integrated planning
Conflict resolution

Strategy
Vision

Scorecards
Organisational structure

vorking
usiasm

Customer relationships
Social responsibility

uditing
scue plan

Results
Marketing and sales

Business intelligence
Research

Differentiation
Creativity

The Enneagram as a systems model

ness theory has for some time welcomed the concept of systems thinking.
languaged as a way to understand the relationship of parts rather than
sing on the parts themselves. When we focus on these relationships we can

often solve problems more effectively than if we just hone in on a part.

An example of this could be an unhappy customer who has been incorrect invoiced. We could easily assume that the problem lies with the invoicing process, but after some investigation we find out that the communication between warehousing, customer services and the accounts department is where the proverbial ball has been dropped. This is an example where utilising the concept of systems thinking can assist people in business to deal with problems in a holistic way rather than just blindly focusing on what might be assumed be the problem.

In my experience of general management, quality systems auditing, human resources and MBA studies, I have garnered insights into how the Enneagram can be used as an effective systems diagnostic tool. Although this book was not solely purposed for business, it might be interesting for those who are employed in an organisation or have their own enterprise to reflect on how the Enneagram can be used in solving business challenges.

Type Eight – The vision and strategic plan are key ingredients for a new venture or to re-engineer or change a threatened business. This requires a strong will leadership and the courage to change the status quo.

Type Nine – The ability to see the bigger picture in planning how the sum of the parts will play a part in making the venture succeed. This also involves ability to mediate when inevitable conflicts arise.

Type One – Accuracy, scorecards, measuring results and the ability to pull all parts together as a project plan are required to ensure that any venture succeeds. Organisational structure is required to ensure accountability and the intelligent flow of activities.

Type Two – Without customers and the ability to care about and exceed their expectations, there is no business. Having a social conscience and paying forward are essential when doing business in South Africa if we are to bring about true transformation.

Type Three – Packaging, promoting, branding and marketing the business to potential customers is as important as the sales function, which involves persuasiveness and achieving results.

Type Four – In world markets which offer so much choice, the ability to differentiate and to always be innovating and creating products and services that will entice customers is vital.

Type Five – Business intelligence with regard to competitors and exploring wider opportunities in the economy means that thorough research takes place which focuses on factual information.

Type Six – It is necessary that all activities are audited to ensure that there is compliance to legislation and that best practices are followed. It is also vital that a rescue plan is formulated when the unexpected occurs, as in the recent global market crashes.

Type Seven – Networking with all stakeholders is essential if the business is to flourish as a triple bottom line entity – being financially, environmentally and socially responsible. Having fun and being enthused is what makes people want to engage with a business – as employees or customers.

When we combine these nine processes we realise that they are all interdependent and essential if a business is to flourish. Some people will be more competent and inclined to focus on specific processes, but ultimately the team or the organisation will need to ensure that all are present within the business systems.

The following chapter presents two assessments which will help you to find your own Enneagram type.

CHAPTER THREE

Finding your tribe or type

IF THE ENNEAGRAM is to be used for self-understanding or for understanding others, an accurate assessment of the dominant personality type is required. A number of assessments have been produced to assist people in finding their dominant type. One of the most reliable was developed by Riso and Hudson called the Riso-Hudson Enneagram Type Indicator, which they promote as a reliable tool for type indicating. They concede that many people are able intuitively to sense their type, but the authors are attempting to complement intuition by verifying the personality types empirically.

However, anyone who is expert in psychometrics will attest to the fact that no test is 100% accurate. I had personal experience of identifying myself initially as an Enneagram type that turned out not to be my true type. This is termed 'mistyping'. The results of two reputable online assessment tests showed that my dominant type was Type Seven, the *Enthusiast*. Despite attending many courses, two based in Europe and one in the US, I was convinced that Type Seven was my type. After some intense debriefing with a wise teacher from Denmark, I was invited to reflect on the descriptions of Type Three, the *Achiever*. I then discovered that this was my true type. This was an arduous experience as I realised that some of the traits of the Type Three were areas of my personality which I was avoiding as they were difficult to own up to. But this knowledge has since helped to really confront these blind spots, make peace with them and embrace the more healthy aspects of my being.

Certain types are more easily confused with others. Types Three and Seven are both assertive types, although Type Three is in the Heart Centre and Type Seven is in the Head Centre. Chapter 13 explains the Centres more fully. When Type Three and Type Seven are both of the sexual instinctual variants (also refer to Chapter 13) they are even more alike. It is important to note that the self-observations and reflections added more value to my self-development and personal growth experience than the outcome of the type itself. However, knowledge of my true type has further assisted me in resolving childhood issues that had previously troubled me. Furthermore, this awareness has assisted

dealing more constructively with conflict situations. This experience has led
e to appreciate that finding the true Centre should be the starting place for
dividuals wanting to establish their Enneagram type.

Other types that can easily be mis-typed or confused are Types One and Five,
vo and Six, Seven and Nine, and Eight and Four. However, all the types have
e potential for mis-typing and individuals should not rely on tests alone. I
ve found one-on-one coaching with an informed Enneagram teacher to be
e most helpful way of assisting people to find their true type.

nding your Enneagram type

stated earlier, our personalities are usually formed by the time we are young
ults. Depending on many factors such as parental nurturing, peer and teacher
luence, material resources and health, we may either have healthy, average
unhealthy personalities reflected by our behaviour. It is in any event helpful
en completing an assessment to think of yourself as a young adult, because
are likely to try to modify our personality type as life circumstances force us
fit in with others as we grow older.

I have devised this assessment from the personality traits that I have observed
st commonly in people who have typed themselves. I have been influenced
Riso and Hudson's *Core Dynamics* (2004) as taught during Part One of
ir Enneagram workshops. Remember that these are traits and we do not
ays know what motivates our behaviour. Only the person with deep inner
owledge can truthfully answer that question, so a test like this will always just
an indicator of type.

My first suggestion is that you draw up a list of your positive and negative
sonality traits. You can even invite a trusted friend, partner or colleague to
this with you – it will give you interesting insights into your behaviour and
as for growth.

Now put this list aside and tick the descriptions that you think fit you most
urately. It is important to remember that we all display most of these traits to
naller or larger extent – so only tick the ones that you believe *really* describe
r behaviour.

Remember to do this test in pencil or another paper so that others may also
able to complete the questionnaire after you.

AN ENNEAGRAM ASSESSMENT

Strong
Resilient – you easily bounce back after difficulties . . . . [

Straight-talking
Others may at times be offended by your direct communication . . . . [

Wilful
Wanting to do things your way, sometimes without consideration to others [

Show anger
Easily express angry feelings – when angry you can sense the heat in
your belly. . . . . [

Resourceful
Will find a way out of difficulty by making a plan and getting others
to support it . . . . ▮

Shrewd
Streetwise in finding solutions and not necessarily following the
conventional way . . . . ▮

Assertive
May walk over others, do not allow others to walk over you and sometimes
you may forget to walk with others . . . . ▮

Inspiring
Can get others to buy into a vision of doing things with your convincing
can-do manner . . . . ▪

Heroic
Can sacrifice self for others, especially when you notice that another has
been treated unfairly . . . . ▪

Territorial
Requiring room to move and control of your own space especially when
others push you into a corner . . . . ▪

If you have identified with most of these traits, you may be a
Type Eight – the *Challenger*

atient
ble to wait for however long it takes for an outcome or response
om others . . . . ☐

elaxed appearance
on't visibly get worked up about things even when those around you are
a froth . . . . ☐

aydream
an get lost in your own thoughts, doodle on paper or just stare at
othing' . . . . ☐

on-reactive
lways first check the facts before reacting to problems or people . . . . ☐

ubborn
ometimes choose to do nothing about a situation in the hope that the
oblem will go away . . . . ☐

rene
njoy peacefulness and the contentment of happy people around you. . . . . . ☐

iplomatic
ill not upset others unnecessarily and will find a way of giving people
e best version of a problem first . . . . ☐

ssive-aggressive
ay show anger in hidden ways, e.g. instead of telling someone you are
gry you do something small which will annoy them . . . . ☐

signed
oid controlling or staging an outcome and rather wait for fate
decide . . . . ☐

sygoing
oid conflict and often negotiate for peace as you prefer to be a nice
son to have around . . . . ☐

ou have identified with most of these traits, you may be a
pe Nine – the *Peacemaker*

Critical
Often criticise yourself and you are inclined to find fault with others ......☐

Perfectionist
If something matters to you, you will ensure that it is perfect.............☐

Idealistic
Holding strong views on how things should be and concerned
with fairness ....☐

Self-disciplined
When committed will push yourself hard to meet your objectives
or standards ....☐

Opinionated
Hold strong views on how things should be and will argue with
conviction ....☐

Impatient
Needing to take action immediately.................................☐

Principled
Having strong belief systems and telling others how things should
be done ....☐

Irritable
Experience levels of stress when things go wrong ....■

Responsible
A strong sense of responsibility and taking care of what matters ....■

Serious
Having a steady intention and not getting sidetracked..................

If you have identified with most of these traits, you may be a
Type One – the *Reformer*

Caring
Concern for others' needs and well-being usually come before taking care
of your own needs .... ☐

Closeness to others
Needing to express warmth by touching others – physically or
emotionally .... ☐

Generous
You really enjoy giving to others and will find different ways to
please people .... ☐

Flattering
You notice nice things about others and you are free in giving others
compliments .... ☐

Empathetic
You sense others' pain and you will give sympathy in a genuine way .... ☐

People pleasing
You sometimes find yourself only focusing on satisfying others' needs ..... ☐

Thoughtful
You are usually firstly concerned with others' happiness .... ☐

Compassionate
You care deeply about others' pain and will find genuine ways to
show this .... ☐

Nurturing
You enjoy taking care of and giving advice to others .... ☐

Selfless
You sometimes feel you have neglected yourself because you have been
too concerned for others .... ☐

If you have identified with most of these traits, you may be a
Type Two – the *Helper*

Competent
When you decide to do something you strive to become masterful . . . . ☐

Performance-driven
You are focused on results and may get impatient with others who
play around when things need to get done . . . . ☐

Charming
You easily use your friendly style to win others over, especially when
they are irritated with you . . . . ☐

Competitive
You will make sure that you give it your all when you want to be the
best when committed . . . . ☐

Confident
When you hold the floor people listen to you and you have a strong belief
in yourself . . . . ☐

Pragmatic
You will find the most practical and easy way to get things done . . . . ☐

Ambitious
Achieving results is so important that you may sometimes even experience
exhaustion . . . . ☐

Adaptable
Can easily change course or fit in with others depending on the
circumstances . . . . ☐

Image conscious
You are aware of how others view you and will make sure you look
appropriate for the circumstances . . . . ☐

Role model
Others often look up to you for your achievements and you thrive on
getting positive feedback from others. . . . . ☐

If you have identified with most of these traits, you may be a
Type Three – the *Achiever*

tuitive

ᴜ can feel or sense things about others which they may not even know
out themselves ....☐

eative

ᴜ enjoy thinking about or doing things differently. This may be in
tistic expression or in the way you live or work. ....☐

notional

ᴜ often feel things deeply and will spend much time making sense of
ᴜr feelings ....☐

aginative

ᴜ use your imagination to heighten your feelings and emotions. ....☐

amatic

ᴜr emotions are felt deeply and this may lead you to act out
ordingly ....☐

ssionate

ɪ feel things deeply and strongly, and will express this to others in
ɪr communication ....☐

rospective

times you are quiet and thoughtful, and you enjoy listening to your
er emotions ....☐

ody

en others hurt or irritate you, you are inclined to retreat until they
ke up with you. ....☐

sitive

often find that others can hurt you even if it is not their intention .....☐

cial

important to you that others see you differently and not just as one
ne herd. ....☐

ᴜ have identified with most of these traits, you may be a
e **Four** – the *Individualist*

Observant
You often notice things which others may ignore or not even be aware of...[

Curious
When something grabs your interest, you make it your business to gain a
thorough knowledge of the subject ....[

Unsentimental
You are able to see things on an entirely objective level – others even say
you lack feelings at times...[

Private
You need to have time by yourself and enjoy time alone with your own a
thoughts and occupation..▮

Preoccupied
Sometimes you can forget that others are there as you are so busy with
own thoughts ....

Independent
You seldom need other people to make you happy and are able to
cope alone...

Exploratory
You enjoy picking things to pieces and finding out how things work........

Expert
You enjoy telling people about things where you have thorough
knowledge..

Foolishness
You easily get irritated by people who think they know how to do things
and then mess up ....

Analytical
People often comment on how you can logically see a situation and
problem solve ....

If you have identified with most of these traits, you may be a
Type Five – the *Investigator*

eliable
nce you are committed, people can depend on you. . . . .☐

utiful
ou will seldom let others or yourself down when there is a job to be
one. . . . .☐

oubting
u often don't trust yourself and will ask others' advice when making
·cisions . . . .☐

orrying
·u spend much time and energy thinking about what can go
ong. . . . .☐

utious
u are careful about committing to new friendships or ideas which are
·t tested. . . . .☐

yal
ice you have a friend it is for life – your friendships often go back many
irs. . . . .☐

aming
hen things go wrong you become very irritated with yourself or others. . .☐

gative
hers often say you see the downside of things rather than the upside . . . .☐

spicious
u are often wary about others' true intentions . . . .☐

epared
u make sure that you are armed with a back-up plan for life
iations . . . .☐

·ou have identified with most of these traits, you may be a
·e Six – the *Loyalist*

Spontaneous
You easily respond to opportunities – especially if they involve fun and
laughter . . . . [

Adventurous
You enjoy exploring new things and may sign up before you have really
researched . . . . [

Superior
You hold onto your opinions and you can sometimes be perceived as
superior by others. . . . . [

Scattered
You often lose things, especially when you are under stress . . . . [

Impulsive
You find it difficult to sit things out – wanting things to happen instantly . . ▮

Escaping
You are good at finding an easy way out of difficulty or pain . . . . ▮

Excessive
You may overindulge, e.g. food, substances or experiences, usually leaving
the party last . . . . ▮

Optimistic
You are able to see the bright side of life, and get irritated by
'wet blankets'. . . . .

Outgoing
You are completely at ease in meeting new people and expressing
yourself . . . .

Seeking variety
You avoid boredom by enjoying different people, experiences or
places . . . .

If you have identified with most of these traits, you may be a
Type Seven – the *Enthusiast*

ʏping yourself though exemplars

ᵻbserving those who are sure of their Enneagram type can also be a powerful ᵻay of finding your own type. Teachers such as Helen Palmer have demonstrated ᵻis process successfully, by interviewing small groups, or exemplars, of the fferent types, to audiences of students learning about the Enneagram.

The chapters that follow will illustrate each of the nine types through an terview process wherein I have invited an exemplar of a type to answer ᵻestions which have been posed in a way to best illustrate the type. Readers ay even be able to identify their type by reading these interviews.

You may feel tempted to rush and read the chapter that applies to the type ᵻu have most identified with in the assessments in the previous chapter. This understandable, but be sure to read the others as carefully as you may find ᵻher insights into yourself, and you will certainly find among the exemplars ᵻe personalities of your family, friends and colleagues.

Each of the type chapters contains some practical advice on the triggers that ᵻing out your blind spots and how best to turn them into strengths through ᵻf-awareness. This is followed with tips on how best to get on with each type if ᵻu are the 'other' in their life. This could be a colleague, partner, spouse, child, ᵻnily member or friend.

I have treated the personality types as if they were healthy and on a positive path ᵻdevelopment. However, when people are seriously traumatised by childhood or ᵻer life stresses they may fall into pathology. This pathology is briefly described ᵻ each type as it may be useful when we are able to recognise these behaviours ᵻd encourage people in need to seek professional psychiatric help.

CHAPTER FOUR

Type Eight – the Challenger

THE CHOSEN ANIMAL THAT SYMBOLISES THE TYPE EIGHT is the lion as it is the king (or the queen if a lioness) of the jungle, showing strength and resilience.

Can you tell us of a time when you needed to be resilient – how did you show your strength?

Five years ago my mother's colon cancer returned. She bravely underwent colostomy and chemotherapy, to no avail. Over a period of three months she deteriorated. Soon she was too weak to get up at all. Her pain was unbearable and the time between doses of morphine got shorter and shorter. To see my beautiful mum losing her dignity in such excruciating pain was absolutely shocking. I had never felt so hopeless.

To get a grip, I had to try to take charge of things. I shopped for morsels to tempt her to eat: a prawn or two, strawberries. I hired nursing equipment, I made sure her will was in order and filed it. I paid all her bills, sorted out the medical aid, attacked cupboards and threw out junk. As the situation got unbearable, my sister and I discussed the relief of euthanasia ...

And then I knew I had to summon my brother from Tanzania. He arrived and she died the following morning.

People sometimes describe you as a straight-talker. How may this have offended others in the past?

A few years ago I met up with one of my classmates from school, and she told me that I had been very bossy as a teenager! *Moi?* Never!

I merely take charge if something needs to be done and no one seems to be making a plan.

ou are known to be keen to get things done your way. Can you describe how ais happens?

cannot bear ditherers: people who cannot assess a situation, come up with ternatives and make a decision about a plan of action. I think I often get things one my way because I'm quick off the mark with possible solutions, and I tend take charge (unless there is someone more persuasive than I am). Others ten end up following me, I suppose either because I do tend to take charge because they do not want to stick their neck out and take responsibility emselves. I have been told that I can also be quite forceful – which is rather ful really. It is not my intention to offend anyone or be undemocratic.

I have, however, learned to restrain myself (somewhat) over the past few years, be less controlling, to give others a chance to express their ideas and to listen to em. I have come to realise that the best decisions are often made after weighing the combined wisdom of the group. And, of course, it goes without saying that e also improves one's chances of support if others in the team feel as though ey have been consulted and are party to the decision and plan of action.

hen you experience anger, how do you experience it physically?

generally takes me some time to get angry, but when I do, I have a terribly rce temper. I feel a surge of heat rush through my chest and I have been own to make some harsh and cutting remarks (sometimes things I have retted later). But once I have blown my fuse it is all over! I move on. I never r grudges or mull over things for days.

Witnessing cruelty, injustice or sheer stupidity (a subjective judgement, I ow) can bring out this reaction in me.

have been working on controlling my blowouts, which I know are juvenile and cceptable, and I'm happy to say that I haven't thrown many hissies recently!

en faced with life challenges, how do you go about finding solutions?

n an optimist, and always believe there is a solution to a problem. I don't up easily. I think I'm a good lateral thinker and will look at a problem from ny angles. I see adversity as a challenge, and of course I love to win!

ne may even say that you can 'walk over others'. How has this shown up in r life?

ave had to defend myself at the CCMA [an industrial tribunal] when lenged by an unhappy employee.

When cornered by another you can be streetwise in getting out of the conflic Can you think of a time when this happened to you?

I have sweet-talked my way out of trouble many times in my life ... mac people see the world from my point of view. Like when I hitchhiked home fro. university and was taken for a joyride by the driver! I have even persuaded traffic cop that he really didn't 'need' to fine me.

You have the gift of inspiring others. How does this happen?

I think once I commit myself to something I believe in, I give it all I've got. I g passionate about making a success of whatever I have put my mind to. I gues get so enthusiastic about the possibilities and way forward that I can often s an idea to the rest of the team.

When necessary you may sacrifice yourself for others. In what circumstan has this happened?

I feel passionate about most things in life, which probably makes me impossi to live with! I cannot tolerate injustice, and will always fight for the underd and what I believe in. At university I took part in NUSAS [a student unio rallies, and I was one of several charged for protesting outside John Vors Square against the apartheid regime. I taught in 'black schools' in the 1970s, and the powers that be refused to re-employ me later as I was seen a 'troublemaker'. During the 1980s I belonged to the End Conscription Campa and the United Democratic Front (UDF). I probably have a criminal recor some police file!

You do not enjoy others taking over your space. How do you react when occurs?

It depends on the context. If I believe in the mission I will give it everything got. If I don't, I can withdraw and move onto something else.

Observations of Type Eight – the Challenger

- The resilience of the Type Eight is well described in how this one dealt w her mother's illness. Even though she was emotionally devastated, her wa of coping was to take action by doing the practical things that needed to done for her mother in her time of illness.
- She readily accepts her bossiness and confirms this in how her friends perceived her behaviour as a teenager. It is interesting to note that throu

developing her self-awareness she now sees that she can get more support from others if she allows for consultation.

- Type Eights are concerned about fairness and are likely to react strongly if there is unfairness. This Type Eight was willing to risk her freedom for fighting against the unfairness of apartheid as a student. Many students were imprisoned for this activity during this time, but she showed up as fearless and heroic in fighting for her principles. Type Eights will also readily take up the cudgels for the underdog and they will be fierce in the way they protect and defend.
- Making light of the time when she was kidnapped when hitchhiking is typical of the Type Eight not giving into fear when threatened by a potentially very dangerous situation.

Trigger points to becoming self-aware of your blind spots

- Recognise that you are more intense and robust than most other people. Tone down 'your volume' so that you do not intimidate others.
- When you feel the warmth of anger rise in your belly area, focus on your breathing to prevent yourself from having an outburst which you may later regret.
- You need not be responsible for everyone. Empower others by encouraging them to learn to take care of themselves.
- People are not always intent on tripping you up. When you start seeing 'enemies', rein yourself back and consider that you may creating the 'spooks' in your own mind.
- It is okay to show your vulnerable side to others. When you are sufficiently relaxed to do this people will open up to you and you will gain their trust.

How we can bring out the best in Type Eights

- Because Type Eights are tough, they enjoy being challenged with truth and conviction.
- Underneath the tough exterior they have a marshmallow heart. Appeal to their soft side by giving them positive feedback.
- Resist speaking about Type Eights behind their back. They can take robust feedback but their anger will be aroused if they believe that others have been disloyal to them.
- Don't take things too personally when they do their straight-talking. If you need to confront them, do so when they are relaxed and preferably alone.

- Recognise their gentle side and how they will often stand up for the weak or powerless.

If Type Eights have experienced some severe trauma in life they may develop antisocial behaviour which is characterised by aggression, lying and manipulation.

At the highest level of development Type Eights become truly courageous and heroic role models in their families, workplaces and communities.

CHAPTER FIVE

Type Nine – the Peacemaker

THE CROCODILE IS THE CHOSEN ANIMAL that symbolises the Type Nine as it can zone out in the sun for hours – its heartbeat slows down to nothing – but if tempted it can be fierce with its prey.

You have the ability 'to sit things out' rather than push for an outcome. Can you think of an example of this happening in your life?

Early on in my career I battled tremendously with managing areas where I had no specialist knowledge. A specific situation I remember clearly was when asked to procure three laptops for the group CEO. I was so focused on finding the appropriate specifications for the laptop at a competitive price that it took me two months of research and non-delivery to acquire them.

You have a tendency to chill out. How best do you experience this?

My favourite activity in the evening (during the week), if I am not engaging in a team sport, is to lie on the couch at home and watch television. This affords me the opportunity to simply chill out and since I can multitask I take in most of what I am watching and reflect on the day gone by and on any stresses in my life simultaneously.

When others get upset you are able to remain calm under pressure. Can you describe this happening?

I have an ability to see the strengths and weaknesses of most arguments and life situations. I am easily able to assess underlying reasons for specific behaviours or individuals or groups.

An example of being able to stay calm under pressure was when earlier in the year I took my four-year-old son on a bike ride. Soon, before we had to descend an extremely big hill, he pulled his brakes too tightly and I did not realise it at the time, but he had lost his confidence. When he started the descent, he started screaming

and I immediately realised the magnitude of the danger and jumped into action
rode up next to him and just told him to stay calm and keep the wheels of the bi
straight, which was the only action possible that would have ensured his safety.

**Most people immediately react to situations. You are more inclined to fir
the facts before you react. Please give us an example.**
I try to always get all the information and points of view before jumping
any conclusions. Many managers play the 'blame game', i.e. pointing fingers
others before all the facts are taken into consideration. When encountered wi
such gripes I always insist on getting all the information/sides of the story fir
Usually I call a meeting of the interested parties to ensure that I get the full sto
in an attempt to understand exactly the nature of the problem. Only then car
go ahead and find the best solution. My philosophy is that anybody can make
mistake and it is critical that the process is assessed and improved if necessar

Type Nines have been found to be stubborn. How do you experience this?
If I do not want to do something and have expressed this, then I will not
remember back to when I worked for a bank in London. I had repeated
said to the management that I wanted to leave as the job I was doing was n
stimulating. They kept indicating that I needed to work another week. They ha
kept a retainer fee which I would only receive after six months and I had on
been there for three months. After the third or fourth week, I got my timeshe
signed, took my jacket and walked out the building as I did not feel that th
had taken my request seriously!

What situations in life do you find most serene or peaceful?
Nothing beats going to sea with our seven-metre boat to crayfish, fish or div
Being on the sea and in the sun is relaxing, and the activity is so far remov
from life's routines that it enables my mind to stop thinking about everythi
that may be stressing me out at the time. When I depart from the harbour ar
go around the harbour wall, my mind instantly relaxes.

How do you use your diplomacy when faced with tricky situations?
I usually assume a calm voice and request all parties to stick purely to the fac
I try to assess quickly what the real reasons are for a specific behaviour of tl
parties involved. Often I would push back and/or coach parties to an agreement
do think I have an ability to assess any situation in a balanced manner.

In what way have you been passive-aggressive towards another (i.e. not visibly reacting but finding a subtle way to show your displeasure)?
When I was younger if somebody annoyed or challenged me, I would make sure that I got my own back. I would do this by knowingly irritating or embarrassing them. I also had an absolute inability to let an argument be.

What examples would your friends use in illustrating your 'easygoing' nature?
I am very flexible and generally can adapt to any situation with any group of people.

When have you resigned yourself to an outcome when you perhaps should have stood your ground?
Early on in my career I was on contract. During this period my line manager said to me that I would definitely get a bonus at the end of the year, but that he would not put anything in writing and that I would have to trust him. When the time came, he reneged on the promise. I was extremely angry and disappointed, but could not get myself to follow through with any appropriate action, which reasonably would have been to leave the company. In hindsight, it was perhaps my ability to have a balanced view of future prospects at the company that made me not resign out of principle.

Observations of Type Nine – the Peacemaker

Most people would agree that to take two months to procure a laptop is procrastination. At the time this Type Nine probably did not see this behaviour as procrastination, but looking back he objectively calls this incident 'non-delivery'.

Type Nines can have a tendency to be either physically or emotionally lazy, but this Type Nine is physical and enjoys team sports. He does, however, enjoy his TV time when he can just zone out and reflect on his day while watching the programme.

This healthy Type Nine also describes how he finds peace and calm by being out on a fishing boat, hanging out with his friends and using being close to nature as a way to be in touch with himself and to de-stress from the business of his work and family demands.

Finding the balance and seeing both sides of any argument is important to Type Nines. This Type Nine describes this well in how he will measure the strengths and weaknesses and hear out both parties' version by calling a meeting before he makes any decisions.

Trigger points to becoming self-aware of your blind spots

- Listen to yourself when you are talking in circles – stop and think about what it is you want to say and say it, and then stop talking.
- Sometimes you have to take sides on a debate – follow your gut feel, make the decision and move on.
- It is okay to be angry – voice your concerns with 'I' statements. Swallowing your anger will cause you more stress in the long term.
- You are also entitled to have things your way – learn to state what it is that makes you happy instead of always giving in to others.
- When you are tempted to sit in front of the TV for too long, get physical in a way you enjoy – not what you 'should' be doing.
- It is good for you to ponder about your heart's desires. When you feel dazed, place your hand on your heart and then answer your question.

How we can bring out the best in Type Nines

- Sometimes Type Nines need a gentle nudge to get things done when they are in procrastination mode. As long as you do not nag or give them a long to-do list.
- When they are being indecisive, help them by narrowing the issues to be decided on and don't leave the discussion until they have committed.
- Type Nines avoid conflict so encourage them to verbalise their true feelings so that they do not swallow anger and find a way to express their views.
- They are usually humble so you should encourage them to explore their talents and show the world what they have to offer.
- They need 'zoning-out' time and should be left to enjoy recouping their energies in whatever way they find restful.

If Type Nines have experienced some severe trauma in life they may develop dependent personality disorder (DSM-IV). This is characterised by difficulty in making independent decisions and overly dependent behaviour.

At the highest level of development Type Nines become alive and alert themselves – truly awake to life and its possibilities.

CHAPTER SIX

Type One – the Reformer

THE REFORMER, TYPE ONE, is symbolised by the bee, as the honeycomb is made with perfection, and bees are industrious and will sting if threatened.

How do you experience being critical with yourself?
I tend to be critical of what I need to achieve, especially if I am focused on it. I enjoy achieving goals and as a result I can be critical of myself when an outcome is not to my liking. This may not always be consistent with how others see the same outcome but perhaps it's because I set very high standards for myself. However, I can vary between two extremes. I can at times also have a very carefree attitude, where what happens really doesn't matter and my enjoyment is more about the journey of discovery rather than the outcome. In general, I tend to keep my criticisms of myself to myself rather than share them with others.

In what areas of your life do you enjoy having perfect order?
At this point it would be my work, career and studies or, as I like to joke about it, my 'Monday to Friday' life! I suppose that it's not that I enjoy perfect order but I like a sense of control, stability and normality in what I'm trying to achieve so that the end point is clear. In my personal life it's another story altogether… I enjoy the element of surprise and not knowing what will happen next and especially not having any order in what I say or do! My partner usually refers to me as *deurmekaar* (muddled) so I guess it must be true! However, the need to have a sense of order really depends on what my focus is at the time.

You hold strong views on certain issues. What are these issues?
I hold strong views about freedom, individuality, fairness, equality, honesty, friendship and the belief that anybody is capable of doing anything they put their mind to! Of course I'm always interested in listening, learning and trying

other view points on for size – it just doesn't necessarily mean that I'm going to change my views in the longer run!

When you are committed you can exercise high self-control. What have been examples of this?

From a young age it was my goal to travel/work abroad when I was old enough. After studying full time, I landed a great job and was doing really well but never gave up on my goal to travel. I eventually saved enough money to leave and travel abroad. During this time, one of the many sacrifices I had to make was not buying a car so that I could save enough money to travel and pay off my study debt at the same time. This was really hard as it meant that I either had to travel on public transport or negotiate with my older brother for the use of his car. Also, I couldn't just spend money on the latest fashions! Being a fiercely independent person meant that I had to practise high self-control and keep myself motivated. It was a long wait for me but worth it in the end!

Your friends may sometimes think you are opinionated. What are the examples of these opinions?

I can't think of anything specific but friends generally come to me for all sorts of advice. For example, they may want to know where the best restaurant or party is. Other times it's far more serious like whether they should make career move or how to deal with relationship problems. So I guess that I must have very clear opinions about issues which I share freely but I definitely don't like imposing any of these on others, although I have been told that I am very good at influencing people subtly if they don't have the same opinion about something! I'm not often off the mark, though, as people always come back for more advice but maybe that's because I'm intuitive and not just opinionated!

When you are excited about a project you can become impatient. What situations have brought up your impatience?

While studying last year, we were given many projects as part of the Master class. The way we handled these projects was for each member of the group to have an opportunity to be the project leader. I did find that when I was not in charge of the project, I would often get impatient with others for all sorts of reasons. Situations where people are too slow, have very little understanding or don't do their bit can frustrate me and make me impatient. My impatience is result of my intensity rather than the shortcomings of the situation – I think.

me principles are non-negotiable to you. What are these principles and in
hat way do you uphold them for yourself and others?

inciples of self-determination and mutual respect are two that are non-
·gotiable to me. When I come across difficult situations in life, I can become
ry self-determined in finding a solution or way around the problem. In others,
usually encourage people to explore more alternatives before they give up. I
hold my principle of mutual respect in the way I interact with others and my
vironment. My philosophy is to treat others in the same way that they treat me
and of course when people disrespect me it's hard for me not to do the same!

though you can display a fun side, you also have a very serious side. How
es this seriousness show itself?

y serious side tends to show itself in my decisions or choices about issues that
 important to me. I tend to give a lot of thought, emotion and energy before
nake a decision or choice and I enjoy analysing different scenarios before I
 comfortable with my final decision or choice. My seriousness shows itself
en I'm on my own rather than when I'm around others. I suppose that this
because I prefer people to be comfortable with me on a light-hearted level
her than on a serious one.

portant things in life will earn your responsibility. What are these things
d how do deal with them?

ccess, money, experiences and learning earn my responsibility. I spend a lot
time and energy in trying to achieving these and to be happy with the end
ults. The level of success and wealth of experience are a source of motivation
me and they drive my decisions and choices. In terms of people, my family
d friends come easily or naturally to me – they have never really been a
uggle and because of that I don't tend to see them as 'my responsibility'.

en stressed, you can show signs of irritability. How often do you experience
 and what triggers this irritability?

e to operate under a healthy level of stress and I guess this is all the time….
ve what is referred to as 'nervous energy' and I need to be juggling different
s at the same time. I can't stay put for long. I guess what triggers my irritability
eeding to do much more with my time. I like to check off my mental list
 what needs to be done and see that I am actually getting somewhere. My
tability is caused when I'm not moving fast enough.

Observations of Type One – the Reformer

- This Type One equates being critical with setting high standards for herself. Although she is driven and sets herself high aspirations, she also has a carefree side – her weekend self and her friends seeing her 'muddled'. Healthy Type Ones engage with the fun aspects of the Type Seven. This is illustrated in Chapter 13 as the Type One integrates with the link to Type Seven.
- Type Ones are highly principled and this is evidenced by the Type One clearly articulating the principles that she holds dear, i.e. freedom, fairness, equality and mutual respect.
- Having clear goals is important to Type Ones and they will make big sacrifices to achieve their goals. This was evidenced in how she made material sacrifices to meet her aspirations to travel and work overseas.
- Type Ones may view life as a *project plan*. Here the Type One describes how she checks things off on her list and if things do not move fast enough she may become irritable. This demonstrates how Type Ones can be quite hard on themselves.

Trigger points to becoming self-aware of your blind spots

- When you start to feel irritable, slow down and listen to your inner 'judge'. The judge is most likely being unnecessarily critical of you or of others.
- As soon as the word 'should' pops in your head, think about who is really speaking to you. Might it be your parents or some other authority figure?
- When you set yourself unrealistic targets, be reminded that the only perfection is in nature and that you are a human who can only learn from mistakes.
- Be aware that you might rob others of the chance of learning when you try to do everything yourself because you think you are the only one who can do things right.
- Find a fun or creative way to unwind with friends, art or in nature to stop yourself from living life too seriously.

How we can bring out the best in Type Ones

- Be mindful of how you give Type Ones feedback – they are already very self-critical and react sensitively to receiving more criticism.
- They usually have strong opinions about how the world should be and how people should behave. Just hear them out and then state your opinion clearly without taking them on personally.

Encourage Type Ones to delegate or find help when they are over-committed. They have trouble trusting others to do things for them in case they do it wrong.

Type Ones can take things very seriously so invite them to lighten up, share a joke and be easier on themselves.

Always be direct with Type Ones as they will find even a white lie difficult to tolerate.

Type Ones have experienced some severe trauma in life they may develop ᴐsessive-compulsive personality disorder (*DSM-IV*). This is characterised by ᴣid ways of relating to others, perfectionist tendencies, lack of spontaneity and ᴄcessive attention to detail.

At the highest level of development Type Ones find inner grace and wisdom ᴛruly able to give clarity to the world.

CHAPTER SEVEN

Type Two –
the Helper

THE CHOSEN ANIMAL THAT SYMBOLISES THE TYPE TWO is the elephant – it
nurturing and cares deeply about other members of the herd. Its inclusi
instinct ensures that everyone's needs in the herd are heeded – young and ol

**You are known to have concern for others' needs and well-being. How do y
demonstrate this in your life?**
I always try and keep in touch and make a point of remembering things that a
important to others. I belong to a group at our church that works for the nee
in the community.

**You find it easy to express warmth to others. How does this expression sh
itself?**
I love to smile and laugh. One of my favourite ways of expressing myself is
sharing a big warm and sincere hug. Perhaps a touch on the shoulder, arm
hand. I love cooking and baking – I do this with love and then like to shar
with others. My late father taught me to cook. I will always remember our fi
lesson when he said, 'The first thing you put in your pot is love' and if you do
do it with love, then don't do it at all.

**You are typically very generous to others. What examples are there of t
generosity and what motivates you to be generous?**
I regularly have friends or family around for a meal or tea. I am usually
family member that has the family day and arranges it. I give of my time
those that need it, even if it's just to listen with a genuine ear. I freely share
knowledge and have learnt that the more you give the more you get back
other ways. Giving is by far a greater pleasure that receiving, especially wl
you see the happiness and joy that it brings to others.

The motivation is that I love peace, harmony and happiness. I cannot function ell unless I feel this in my life. Also, I love people and need them around me.

ou find it easy to compliment others. In which ways do you do this?
irstly with sincerity and from the heart. It could be so many different ways, but me examples are complimenting a colleague for coming up with something at I think is a good idea or for a job well done; highlighting people's strengths d making them feel good; saying so if I'm enjoying a meal that has been ooked for me or simply a cup of tea that my husband has made for me; sending text message or email of thanks and praise; telling my children regularly that ey are wonderful children and parents, and praising them for their success.

I'm very big on saying thank you and acknowledging what has been done cause it's very important to me to be thanked when I have done something r someone. I think it's important – good manners and very necessary.

hen you sympathise with others, they feel that it is genuine. How do you do is that it is so well received by others?
;ain, from my heart and with sincerity. I try to feel/imagine their pain. With me things in life it can be to my disadvantage because I have maybe reacted th my heart and not my head. I am a very sensitive person and sometimes e too much to heart.

ere are times when you put others' needs before your own. This can relate your partner, family, colleagues, friends or even your pets. How does this ppen?
ie example is when one of my very close and longstanding dear friends (a gle mother) had no stove or microwave and was trying to cook and warm rything in an old electric frying pan. I felt so badly for her and wanted to and help. So after some thought, I took her to a big chain-store under some se pretence that I was pricing some stuff. Then after looking around I told her choose one of the two microwaves that was on offer. She was in shock and belief, and started crying. It took a little while for reality to set in. There was nething that I had planned to buy with this money for my home but in my rt I knew that she needed this microwave more than I needed what I wanted. husband (as always) supported my decision, which made the experience so ch more special.

It is important to you to know that others are happy. How do you go about ensuring this?

Always keep in touch with family and friends and then if there is anything that needs to be done or said, I do my best to do just that. Perhaps if a friend needs to offload I will invite her to come around for coffee, a meal or maybe a 'chick flick'. Then we have a good girls' evening and normally feel much better afterwards.

I also enjoy sending out uplifting text messages to friends or family that may need it or just because it's appropriate for them. Often they will say, 'It's just what I needed today'.

When others are in pain, you are able to care for them deeply. What examples have there been for you of this happening?

My husband had a major operation and was hospitalised three times in a period of five to six weeks. I was back and forth to the hospital afternoons and evenings. Then when he came home I would rush home at lunchtimes to be with him for a little while and attend to his needs while shopping, cooking and working full time. I was completely drained but because I care so deeply it just felt natural to do all these things and I just kept going.

Right in between all of this my brother-in-law (who is single and lives alone) fell and broke his ankle and was hospitalised. We are his only family in South Africa so the responsibility was on us. With my husband being out of commission I tried to see to everything myself. When he came out of hospital he stayed with us for about ten days, so I had two patients at home. By the time my brother-in-law went home I had cooked him approximately a month's meals and frozen them for him. I also gave his place a good spring clean before he moved back in. He also had to be taken back to the hospital for check-ups and physiotherapy.

When my sister had a car accident she phoned me at work to tell me what had happened and was understandably crying and very upset. I offered for to come through to help with anything she may need. She assured me she was fine. Nevertheless I decided to phone my husband and asked him if we could immediately go through to her home to be with her. My husband and I picked up my mom and the three of us went through to my sister's home. She was so grateful and happy to see us. By the time we left her she said that she felt hundred times better and was grateful that she could talk about it. I also saw to it that she had something to eat before we left.

A dear friend of mine lost her husband suddenly. I helped out as much as I ᴊuld, and tried to be a comfort in little ways – phone calls, visits, text messages ꞇd meals. I made sure to keep in touch especially after the funeral and invited ᵉr to spend a weekend with me.

is easy for you to give others advice and to be caring when they are faced ith difficulty. How do you do this?
ʟostly from my own experiences, talking from my heart and by what I truly ᵉlieve. Faith and prayer always help me.

ᵒmetimes you have neglected your own needs because you care so ᵘch for others. How has this happened and did you realise that it may happening?
ꞁo sometimes realise that this happens but it's the love that motivates me. ᵧ leg and knee have been troubling me for quite some time. When I went to ᵣ children on holiday they were aware of it but I always tried to cover up the ᵪtreme discomfort as much as possible so as not to worry them. I did a lot ᴊund the house for them (as mothers always like to do), also treating both ꞁilies with their favourite meals and babysitting our granddaughters. This ᵴ hell on my leg and knee but I battled through it because of the love I have my precious children and grandchildren.

I have struggled with being overweight for many years and often I also put ᴧers' needs before my own where this is concerned. Even when I know that ᴐking or baking something special for others is going to be a big temptation me, I do it anyway because I know that it's their favourite and it makes m happy. Something else that I always find myself doing (again, I think it's ᴧ a motherly thing) is that when packing lunches I normally would give my ᴉband or children the better-looking fruit or the better, nicer, bigger whatever. done with love so it really doesn't feel too difficult.

ᴼservations of Type Two – the Helper
ᴦhis Type Two demonstrates how easy she finds it to give her affection ᴐ others in physical gestures. She also uses the word 'love' regularly ᴧhroughout her responses.

ꞋJpe Twos can easily become self-sacrificial in their need to give to and ᴉupport others. This is evidenced in her spending money planned for her ᴐwn needs on her friend's microwave. When her husband was ill she placed herself under more pressure by taking care of her ill brother-in-law. She also took care of the family despite her leg giving her pain.

- Being strongly connected to others is an important aspect to the Type Two happiness. This is well illustrated in the frequent references to family and friends.
- The Type Two is a heart type, which is explained in Chapter 13 dealing with the Enneagram Centres. This Type Two is able to reflect on how her dominant tendency to rely on her 'heart' rather than her 'head' has not always served her.

Trigger points to becoming self-aware of your blind spots

- Listen to yourself when you are paying others too many compliments. Could you possibly be asking for the favour to be returned?
- Be clear about how you make requests to others. You also need help at times, and hinting will not always get others to understand what you are really asking for.
- When you find yourself thinking too much about how others see you, remember that it is probably your own preoccupation and not even an issue for them.
- You enjoy doing favours for others. Learn to say no if these requests are invading your life choices or making you feel resentful in some way.
- Let go of past hurts as carrying them around becomes a heavy burden which robs you of loving energy which you could be giving on more deserving people in your life.

How we can bring out the best in Type Twos

- Type Twos actually love to be given sincere positive feedback on their accomplishments or appearance.
- They thrive on attention and will appreciate an invitation to hang out do something which grabs their field of interest.
- When they share their feelings, do not rush in with advice. They may just want a sympathetic ear.
- Type Twos also struggle with perceived criticism as they are inclined to take things personally. Find a way to give them feedback which is gentle and diplomatic.
- Type Twos love to give presents and do things for others – however, be mindful that there might well be an expectation for you to reciprocate.

Type Twos have experienced some severe trauma in life they may develop
istrionic personality disorder (*DSM-IV*). This is characterised by excessive
eed for attention, praise, reassurance and approval.

At the highest level of development Type Twos become truly enabled to
ceive and give pure, unambiguous love.

CHAPTER EIGHT

Type Three – the Achiever

THE CHOSEN ANIMAL THAT SYMBOLISES THE TYPE THREE is the chameleo[n]. It changes its colour to adapt to any situation and its tongue will dart out swift[ly] and fiercely if it sees the opportunity to catch a yummy fly.

You pride yourself in being competent and doing many things well. How do[es] this show up?

It's not so much that I do very many things well, but when I decide to [do] something or it really interests me I will try to excel. So as a young girl I start[ed] horse riding on our farm and as the interest in riding grew this became t[he] thing that I wanted to be the best at and it became an all-consuming passi[on]. I was devastated when my ponies were sold after my parents divorced. I cou[ld] still have carried on riding at boarding school, but I lost interest as I could [no] longer do this competitively and was unwilling to settle for 'second best'.

So there is a kind of selective choice in what I compete in. If I am not goi[ng] to shine then I may do things in a half-hearted way. It has been a life lesson [for] me to be more dutiful in carrying out the more mundane tasks and not o[nly] focusing on the things that might make me shine in the limelight.

You are performance-driven and focus on the results. What examples a[re] there for you of this tendency?

When people tell me their life stories I find myself becoming impatient. I wa[nt] them to get to the bottom line. It is difficult for me to hear others' pain an[d if] they are long-winded I really have to stay in the moment to hear them prope[rly] rather than being more interested in the outcome of the story.

As a mother I also find I want to know about my children's school results m[ore] than I might want to focus on the learning process and their development. I can [see] that this overzealous need for results can often be expediency for the showines[s of] life rather than wanting to engage with the process and messiness of reality.

ou easily employ charm to win people over. How do you go about this?

harming others has always come to me very naturally. It is not that I consciously
t out to do this but rather that it is a vital way for me to win people over.
eep down I need others' approval and a sure way to get this is to smile and be
arm. I am very good at selling myself in interviews and actually quite enjoy the
xperience. When I pick up on disapproval from others I can be devastated and
ill assume that it was something I did wrong rather than seeing the situation
ore objectively. When I stand back I will often see that the other person's reaction
uld have been due to their having experienced a bad day or not agreeing with
e issue and actually had nothing to do with their opinion of me.

When I want to get action from service providers I will always employ charm
a way of getting my needs met. When confronted with poor service, this
arm can easily turn to hostility if I am not self-aware.

When faced with conflict I always use charm first to disarm 'the enemy'. With
arm I also employ reasonability as my second arrow in the quiver, rather than
emotional argument.

u enjoy competition. How does this materialise in your life?

is not always about me being competitive. I love it when my children excel
d I might suffer silently when they lose at something they have set their hearts
. Likewise, when my husband surfed competitively, I really cringed when he
s judged last in a heat.

In business I want our organisation to be the best in its field and can become
ite dismissive of the competition. Even when people leave us to join an
position company, this feels like we have somehow lost in a race. I rejoice
en ex-employees return to us because this means we have in some way 'won'
we are then perceived to be 'the employer of choice'.

**u are naturally confident and have a strong belief in yourself. How is this
monstrated?**

ve always found it easy to stand up in front of others and present information.
a very young girl I naturally enjoyed the stage and later at school excelled in
ating issues in front of an audience. Joining Toastmasters seems strange to
as this is a competency which is so natural to my way of being.

When life has challenged me I have always been able to respond with energy
force knowing that if I tackle problems systematically they will be resolved.
ck empathy for people who sit back and allow themselves to be victims of

their circumstances. It was quite a surprise for me to learn that not everyone sees the world in this way and that I needed to have more compassion and intelligence to accept others' structure of interpretation.

You have strong beliefs in doing things in the most practical way. How do you go about this?

Whenever I am faced with a challenge my first reaction is to unpack the situation and find realistic step-by-step ways to solve them. People who come to me with life problems are usually advised to do things rather than mull over their problems. It has been a huge lesson that not everybody wants practical advice to sort out their life issues, but sometimes people just want to be listened to. I sometimes feel that I carry this huge toolbox around with me, and for every situation in life I will find the spanner that will fix it.

Recently when I heard of the death of someone dear, I immediately started suggesting practical considerations regarding death benefits and funeral arrangements. It only struck me afterwards that I was doing this to avoid the emotional hurt for me and the person I was conversing with at the time.

It is important in your life that you achieve your goals and that others do the same. What have been examples?

Owing to family circumstances I was unable to complete my school education although I was considered to be an above-average student. I have been able to secure positions with good employers and have in this way been able to study part time. In this way I have completed a diploma course, an Honours degree, Master's and a doctorate degree in my field of study.

Currently I have less personal ambition but seek to instil in my children and the young people whom I mentor a yearning to achieve the best that they can through learning, compassion for others and smart work. It is difficult to understand how people do not use their full potential and I am impatient with those who choose to live a life focused only on idle distractions. I try not to judge those who are privileged but do nothing to support the poor and previously disadvantaged people in our country.

You can easily take on different roles depending on circumstances. How do you do this?

I find it easy to adapt to any social gathering and love the opportunity to engage with different cultures and nationalities. I have worked in very different industries and had no challenge in making the transition.

In my work I am easily able to change roles from legal representative to coach to facilitator to strategist to administrator to adviser to clown.

My wardrobe has three distinct categories. Work life, relaxation and classic-hippie for going out. And never will they be mixed!

I can hear myself taking on the accent and way of being when I am travelling. When in Ghana I had my hair braided and in Bali I dreamt of becoming a gentle spiritual being – 'you are one of us' – but it is also a genuine curiosity of wanting to be in another's skin.

Your type is often seen as the archetypal American who is image-conscious. Is this true for you?

This is an embarrassing question but when I am really honest I have to say there truth. There is value in my job title and at times I will use my 'Doctor' status to impress others in order to achieve an objective.

I have always enjoyed driving cars which have brand status and currently I drive a Mini Sidewalk. My appearance is important and I will not leave home not feeling okay about my make-up, hair and dress.

My husband was given a wardrobe make-over soon after we committed to a permanent relationship. It is sweet that after 20 years he still checks in with me see if he is dressed appropriately for an occasion. Similarly it is important to me that we live in a good neighbourhood. I do not consider myself a snob, but I will not spend lengthy time with those who deplete mental energy.

How do you feel about being a role model to others?

It makes me happy to think that others might be inspired by me in some way. I have always set out to be the kind of mother whom my children will learn from but also be comfortable to introduce to their friends.

Volunteering to be a mentor to others and steering my junior work members to being the best that they can be for themselves, others and their communities important. It is embarrassing when I get direct accolades from others and I prefer to know that when I have been an example to others it has been through authenticity rather than in having been 'showy' in a superficial manner.

I still need to let go of wanting to convince others of my perspective when I believe that an issue really matters, and allowing things to just be and thus keeping relationships intact. That would mean another step to being a real role model.

Observations of a Type Three – the Achiever

- Type Threes avoid failure at all cost. This is evidenced in how this Type Three was only interested in competing on a horse that she could rely on but lost interest in riding a horse that was unknown and would possibly make her appear to be a failure.
- If Type Threes are not able to compete directly they will often project their ambitions on their family. This is illustrated in how the Type Three needs her children, her husband and even her organisation to be success stories.
- Although situated in the Heart Centre, Type Threes often suppress their emotions in their business of achieving their agendas. This Type Three tells us how hard it has been to deal with others' pain caused by death and in her learning to become a better listener.
- Not all Type Threes are flashy and brand-obsessed. Their tastes in material things will depend on their values. This Type Three enjoys the Mini brand but other Type Threes might choose the best bike, cool surfboard or sporting the latest hair style.

Trigger points to becoming self-aware of your blind spots

- When you feel the urge to beat everyone else at something, stop and think why this is necessary. Try to settle for being your own best.
- Catch yourself when you are moulding yourself to those around you. If your motive is to manipulate the situation, step back and be your authentic self.
- Find the things in life that bring you true joy rather than just rushing after the next accomplishment on your long to-do list.
- Watch out for the small lies or exaggerations you may tell for effect. People like you for what you have to offer and you do not need to offer more than what is already there.
- Do not spend too much energy on worrying about material things – your appearance or the latest gadgets. Rather focus on your relationships and being true to yourself.

How we can bring out the best in Type Threes

- Type Threes want to be appreciated for the gifts they bring to relationships and not only for their achievements.
- Do not ignore them – when there is a reason for their being left out, explain it and they will understand.

- When Type Threes fail at something they take it very hard. Give them encouragement and remind them of their worth in the ways that really matter.
- Type Threes sometimes sound tactless because when things are wrong they want to fix them. Deep down they mean well, so do not be offended by their directness.
- Sometimes they get so involved with their 'doing' in life that they neglect their 'being'. Encourage them to slow down and observe what they really are feeling.

f Type Threes have experienced severe trauma in life they may develop narcissistic personality disorder. This is characterised by the adoption of an inflated self-image, and demands for attention and admiration.

At the highest level of development Type Threes become visionary and able to accept and appreciate the simple gifts of life.

CHAPTER NINE

Type Four –
the Individualist

THE CHOSEN ANIMAL THAT SYMBOLISES THE TYPE FOUR is the cat because she can be mysterious, graces us with her presence when it suits her and can be content in her own company. This is the only domestic animal that demonstrate being different to the other eight animal symbols chosen from wildlife.

You are able to feel or sense things that others might not notice. Can you think of an example of this?
The best example I can think of is my approach to problem-solving. When I'm confronted with a problem, I approach it intuitively, not always following a linear way of thinking, but 'sensing' what the solution might be. Sometime people wonder how I come to certain conclusions and then, years later, remark on how accurate I was.

I also have an intense appreciation for the natural world. I feel spiritually uplifted when I'm in nature, where I sense a deep connection to something powerful and mysterious. I'm constantly taking mental 'snapshots' – of a floc of geese flying over a full moon, a ladybug crawling up my arm… I relish in these simple pleasures. While I'm intensely aware of my emotions and the natural world, I'm quite oblivious when it comes to material things (I seldom remember what kind of car people drive) and practical matters (like filling in my tax return!). I've had to learn the hard way as it never came naturally to me. I have often envied people like my brother, an actuary, who seems so together while my life always seems chaotic.

Working has taught me how important it is to be 'streetwise' and to emerge from my 'dream world'. I feel I am a more balanced person now. I will always be a dreamer with my head in the clouds, but with both feet firmly planted on the ground! I am always on the look-out – you could say I'm even on a quest – to find 'what really matters' and 'what is truly real' and important in life, to find that lost sense of connection. Consequently, what others consider important

ometimes consider trivial. I despise pretences and superficiality. You won't
ch me in MacDonald's! I'm more likely to be in a sidewalk bistro with art on
: walls and French music playing from an old gramophone...

On the other hand, life has taught me not to judge people too harshly, and
t to shut my eyes to what I consider 'ugly'. Often these things have their
n beauty. I am very driven and set high standards for myself, but I'm not
ngry for material things. I'm very ambitious and restless, but my ambition
nothing to do with material things or financial gain, but with more abstract
ngs that can't be seen, like truth, beauty, wisdom. (In another life I would
ely have been a spiritual pilgrim of some sort!). Being very driven, I can be
y hard on myself and self-critical.

**pressing your creativity matters to you. What avenue have you found for
s expression?**

act my creativity has been a side of me that I have repressed for many years
it's taken me a long time to truly accept that part of me, which is such a
l part of my being. For so long I stifled my creativity for fear of being seen
laky' and suffered as a result.

started writing when I was a child – mainly fictional stories where my
asy life could take flight, and poetry. I literally have boxes filled with writing
ny cupboard! I'm always writing – even if it's just scribbling in my journal.
only been in the past year or so that I've managed to find a way to make
ing from writing. It's very satisfying to know I can use my creativity in a
tical way. What I love about writing is that it allows me to express my inner
d, making the unseen seen.

Vriting for magazines is good for me because I can be creative and
ospective, but it also 'pulls' me out of my headspace and into the 'real world'.
act I've learnt that engaging with people and reality can often inspire my
ive life. It's important for me to have a balance.

**mes you feel things very deeply. How do you sense this physically and
t are situations that elicit this?**

nge challenge for me has been learning how to manage my stress levels.
use I feel things so deeply and pick up on people's emotions, I often
overwhelmed and get burnt out very easily. I tend to act out my feelings
tically – through stomach pains and various other physiological symptoms.
use I am so sensitive, many situations can elicit this – seeing a forest that

has been destroyed or a hungry child on the street, or having an argument wi
someone I care about.

I have to be careful about how I internalise my and other people's emotio
because I can literally make myself sick. I often feel fatigued because I ca
around so much emotional heaviness. My husband often has to remind
to lighten up! While I've had to face a lot of challenges in my life, sometin
my pain is self-inflicted. I become caught up in analysing the emotion its
I'm naturally extremely curious about who we are – and what it means to
human. Instead of processing emotions and letting go of them in a heal
way, I can cling to them and ruminate on them, not necessarily becaus
enjoy being maudlin, but because I am so fascinated by my emotions
my body. Sometimes I think I create certain symptoms just so I can le
about them!

While my life has been in constant flux and I've had real challenges to
with, sometimes my pain is in fact more existential than real. Everything m
be going swimmingly in my life, but inside I am in turmoil. I can suffer fr
insomnia as I battle to calm my racing mind. (My husband, who is a very chi
person, often says he can see steam coming out of my ears.)

If the danger for many people is to repress painful feelings, then the da
that the Type Four faces, is to dwell on them for too long. That is why it i
refreshing to meet people who don't take life as seriously as I do. Their ma
is: Just let it be. That is something I find so incredibly hard to do.

**You may use your imagination to heighten your feelings. How does
happen?**

Sometimes I will spend hours ruminating on painful events in my life, repla
the scenes in my mind and reopening old wounds. I can be feeling sad
minute and the next I'll be completely inconsolable, because I've added fu
the fire by dwelling on painful memories. I can end up in a very dark place.
could be feeling a bit hurt about what someone said and then end up in a
just by allowing myself to ruminate too long.

I don't think this is just because I enjoy wallowing in misery, but becaus
so deeply important for me to understand my feelings. I have learnt, how
that sometimes I need to 'shake' myself out of it and to understand tha
feelings aren't necessary a true reflection of reality. I have found therapy
helpful in helping me deal with depression, but the problem is that, as a
Four, I can become addicted to the process not the outcome.

times others have thought you to be dramatic in your response to life
uations. What is an example of this?

example would be smashing our dinner plates when my father passed away.
ly poor husband is now ever-fearful of what I might break next!) It is not that
ntend to be dramatic, but that I want to unearth those feelings and investigate
em. Emotional honesty is very important to me. I'm always asking myself: Is
is real? Is this really meaningful? Again, I've learnt that, in my case, balance
critical. If I get caught up in what is 'real' and what is 'meaningful', I end up
ing in my own private fantasy world.

This extreme, outward display of emotion doesn't happen that often. A subtler
m of being dramatic would be the way I approach my life. As a Type Four, I
n often engage in catastrophic and 'what if' thinking and wallow in self-pity
cause 'nothing good ever happens to me'. For instance, if I can't sleep for one
ght then I'll think, 'Oh I won't be able to go to work tomorrow, and then I'll
e my job, and then I'll end up poor and on the side of the street'… Or I'll be
ogling 'insomnia' and end up frightening myself with all the possible reasons
y I might have it. (Again, a part of this is simply because I'm so fascinated by
· human mind.) Whereas if my husband has a bad night he simply shrugs it
and doesn't think about it too much.

If smashing plates is one extreme of my personality, then bleak depression
nother. Others may see it as self-pitying and narcissistic, but they need to
derstand that these feelings can be very debilitating when they do arise and
e Fours can't simply be told to 'get a grip'. A little compassion and gentleness
help the Type Four emerge from this dark place. But they need to feel that
ers are making an effort to understand them, and not judge them, even if the
ers secretly think they are making too big a deal of it.

t is true that my life has not been easy, but I've learnt to recognise that neither
nyone else's, and often I bring this pain upon myself. I've learned that it is
sible to be happy and for good things to happen to me.

**feel things passionately, deeply and strongly. How best can you illustrate
s?**

re are certain causes that I'm passionate about, particularly protecting our
net, and I also have a soft spot for hungry or homeless children, and dislike
judice of all kinds. In my early 20s I worked for several non-governmental
anisations but seeing orphans and people suffering was incredibly difficult
me, being so empathic. When I listen to people's sad stories, I literally feel

what they are feeling. I decided to move away from welfare work because it w
just too painful, but I still have a deep desire to make a difference in the wo
in some way.

I'm very in touch with my emotions all the time to the extent that I 'wat
myself. A lot of people run away from pain; I run into it! I feel profoun
moved by many things, particularly suffering of any kind. I'm very inspired
those figures in our history who stood up against injustice – from Gandhi
Martin Luther King.

**Sometimes you withdraw and become quiet and introspective. How doe:
feel to you when you are in this space?**
It can feel lonely sometimes. For a while I longed to be extroverted a
confident, and I ended up hurting myself by trying to be someone I'm no
do make an effort to be more sociable, but it can be a challenge because
naturally quite a loner. I tend to hide away from the world and it can be h
for me to trust others because I'm terribly afraid of being misunderstc
and hurt.

Being in my own space – writing, reading, running on the beach – can
wonderful because I sometimes feel overwhelmed by other people's feelir
and can carry their psychic 'baggage'. I'm quite comfortable going to restaura
alone and enjoy my own company. But there will always be that longing
connection.

**Life situations can make you moody and you may then become tempe
mental. What are the triggers for this?**
It can be an external trigger, like work or family stress, but it's not always dicta
by what's happening in my life. Sometimes I get the blues for no reason. Th
doesn't need to be a specific external trigger, although I am acutely sensitiv
many things. My emotional life is like Cape Town weather – four seasons in
day! I don't always reveal my moodiness to people I don't know and have lea
to regulate my moods, but unfortunately my husband does get the brunt of

I have learned that when I do become upset, I shouldn't make myself m
upset about being upset! Instead, I've learned to develop an 'observer self', wh
is always calm and simply watches. That is not to say that there is anyth
wrong with being sad. I believe we should welcome all emotions; instead
very often banish them to the darkest corners of our subconscious where t
can cause more harm. But I tend to go overboard by dwelling on my feelings

uch. That's why I sometimes need my friends and husband to bring me out of
yself, and help me see the lighter side to life.

ou may be easily hurt by others, sometimes unintentionally. Can you think
a time when this happened and how did you react?
friend might say something and I will read something into it, or she might
ticise me and it might bring up all the other hurtful things people have said
out me. (Of course a Type Four never forgets these things!) Often I react by
awling back into my shell and retreating. A part of me sees it as a validation:
u see, no one understands me! But I've learnt not to be so sensitive and
understand that people sometimes say things without thinking, and not
eryone has a hidden agenda.

ere have been times when you have somehow felt different to other people
special. Can you think of examples?
ave felt different my entire life, particularly in settings where I feel my free-
rited nature might not be appreciated, like the corporate environment or any
titutional setting where you're expected to conform to a certain mould. I've
en felt that I'm an alien from another planet and no one really 'gets' me, that
on't fit in anywhere.
At school I was very shy and preferred spending time in my own fantasy
rld – where I could write and read and ponder – to being with other girls,
n though I often wondered what it would be like to have lots of friends and
frivolous and have fun. On the one hand there was this longing to belong;
the other the feeling that I never would. For me, being different doesn't
essarily mean wearing outlandish clothes or being eccentric. It's more about
way I think and feel.
I've learnt that to some extent everyone feels this loneliness – it is part and
cel of being human. We are connected to others, yet we must walk our paths
I die alone. It's a bittersweet sadness.
Now I'm more comfortable in my skin. I know that I am both 'special', but
in some ways I am very similar to others. Instead of always looking at how
n different from other people, I try to focus on our shared traits. This feeling
eing different is two-sided because on the one hand, it's very painful to feel
t you don't fit in, and on the other there's this need to be an individual, to
d out from the crowd, to live your life in a unique way.

While I do feel the need to walk my own path, I do feel an intense need be close to people, to feel that I am part of the human community. But even my marriage, where I feel validated and loved, I still feel very much alone. Type Fours are haunted by a sense of alienation – even from each other.

Observations of a Type Four – the Individualist

- This expressive Type Four describes how painful her emotions can become – to the extent that they can make her feel physically ill. Her difficulty in facing the pain of welfare work, experiencing the blues and being past referenced are all illustrations of how Type Fours are emotionally wired.
- She believes that working helped to wake her from her dream world. Facing the real world of completing tax returns, ordinariness and ugliness are still challenges for her.
- Type Fours often sense that life has in some way been unfair and will envy what others have. This Type Four feels envy for her brother the actuary who seemingly has 'it all together'.
- She has found her creative outlet in writing poetry and other creative writing. She recognises her need for dramatic expression in smashing plates.

Triggers to becoming self-aware of your blind spots

- You can be your own worst enemy when you believe that the world is against you. Find something physical to do, and list your talents and what you appreciate to help you snap out of the gloom of a mood.
- You may not necessarily be an artist, but in some way you have a creative talent. Explore what this is and spend time in an occupation where you can truly find expression.
- When you feel hurt by other people, remember that your emotions are fine tuned, so halve the meaning you got from the other to get perspective.
- Be aware of envying what others have – the 'unfairness' might just be in your imagination and having what others have might not even be in your best interests.
- Catch yourself when you are dwelling in the past rather than being in the moment and appreciating your current opportunities.

How we can bring out the best in Type Fours

- When Type Fours are moody or depressed, do not suggest that they 'snap out of it'. Rather just listen to them, only give gentle advice when they ask for it and accept that this is often how they will experience life.

Appreciate their creativity and be careful about being critical as they will take this very personally.

Type Fours are gifted listeners and do not mind giving advice if you are faced with problems. Appreciate this quality they offer their friends.

Do not feel hurt when they do not appreciate a gift from you – they may have very distinctive tastes and will often change their environment to ensure that it creates a special mood.

They are a very emotional type so be aware, especially if you are more unemotional, that their reactions will often be heightened by the intensity of their feelings.

Type Fours have experienced some severe trauma in life they may develop ɔidant personality disorder. This is characterised by avoidance of social ationships due to fears of rejection.

At the highest level of development Type Fours become emotionally balanced d able to deal with life's challenges with equanimity and self-belief.

CHAPTER TEN

Type Five –
the Investigator

THE CHOSEN ANIMAL THAT SYMBOLISES THE TYPE FIVE is the owl. It is recognis[ed]
to be the animal of wisdom and is a solitary creature.

**You sometimes notice things that others may ignore. Can you think of [an]
example?**

In most instances the cold-water tap is on the right side, and the hot-wa[ter]
tap is on the left side if you face the handbasin or bathtub. Occasionally th[ey]
have been installed in reverse order with the cold water on the left and the h[ot]
water on the right. There appears to be no fixed pattern; however, given that [the]
majority of the population is right-handed they most likely need to open [the]
cold-water tap first with their right hand and therefore cold-water taps sho[uld]
be on the right.

**When something interests you, you can spend much time and energy gaini[ng]
knowledge on the object of interest. How has this happened for you?**

I usually start with gathering information. Just about everywhere I go I wil[l be]
on the search for information on what interests me, for example photogra[phy.]
I would have a look at old and new photographs, cameras and light[ing]
equipment. When it comes to equipment, I ask just about every question [on]
how the equipment works. I really get a thrill understanding how technolog[y is]
used in equipment.

I went to the extent of doing a course on photography when I started ou[t.]
I felt that I lacked the knowledge. Although I had read a lot about photogra[phy]
it felt as though it was not enough. Having hands-on experience seemed like [the]
best way to get more exposure and understanding from like-minded individu[als.]

I had to know everything, leaving no room for the fact that I could h[ave]
missed something along the way in my pursuit of understanding, for all asp[ects]
of photography.

Expenses aside, I purchased all the equipment: external flash, filters and additional macro and zoom lenses, and a tripod. Essentially I felt that I had to have all the accessories in order to get the best photographs. Having equipped myself with the necessary equipment I would go on an outing to take photographs.

Others may become emotional and lose sight of the rational, whereas you will remain objective. How has this happened and what was their reaction to your rationality?

In a disciplinary hearing, I was asked to present the case on behalf of the company. After reviewing all the evidence and weighing it up against the company policy and guidelines, and being attentive to just the facts of the matter and dismissing emotional reasons and reactions, I was able to get to the essential points of the hearing by asking objective questions. Being a practical thinker I was able to reach the end of the hearing quickly. The result of the hearing was in favour of the company.

At the end of the hearing the chairperson was astonished and remarked that I was a judge, jury and executioner all rolled into one and that he wouldn't like to be on the opposing end of a disciplinary hearing to me. The other members of the hearing panel agreed with the chairperson.

It is important to you to have your own space and time to think things through? How do you react when others invade your space?

I generally get irritated or frustrated very quickly. I would wait for others to leave, or look for an alternative space to think. If I can't go anywhere quiet and be alone with my thoughts, it will ultimately result in a delay in important decision-making, until such time as I have had a chance to think the matter through.

When I'm at home I prefer to have the radio or television switched off. This allows me to spend my time thinking rather than have my thoughts interrupted or distracted. I feel that this is the best way for me to focus on my thoughts. Generally, I try to avoid all forms of noise or distractions as far as possible. In this way I will be able to focus on thinking things through.

At times you are almost removed/remote from others as you are so busy in your head with thinking. How does this happen?

Being an observer, only if something is of interest to me will I want to gather or share information on the topic. In most social gatherings people generally engage in small talk, which is of no interest to me. An automatic reaction and a comfort zone for me is to become quiet and withdrawn if I do not have anything to contribute. I would rather spend those moments thinking about the areas that are of great interest to me at that point in time and refine my thoughts. Alternatively, I would be more than comfortable to just observe all the activity around me.

When faced with difficulty you can cope alone and find your solutions. Can you describe this?

I generally start by analysing the situation; in other words, I would take stock of and ascertain what is known and what is unknown using a process of elimination. Having identified the unknowns, I then have direction on what I should gather more information on. I would attempt to gather more information by aligning my thinking to a system. Any system that has one or more inputs will in all probability have one or more outputs. Applying this reasoning I would arrive at a solution(s). Having identified the solution(s) I would first ascertain if a mechanism exists for my situation. If it doesn't I would embark on an exercise to create one to meet my objective.

When problems need to be solved, you unpack and explore how things should work. Please give an example of this.

In the majority of instances when there are problems, there are three possible reasons that caused them. These are:

1. A complete failure due to malfunction
   Solution = replace the malfunctioning item.

2. Changes made to the system which were inappropriate or inaccurate
   Solution = here greater care must be taken to retrace each step up to the point that everything was previously working. Then working through each step going forward, the validity of each action must be tested. In doing so the problem could be identified and the appropriate solution could then be applied or implemented.

3. Lastly, there are new factors which were never previously considered
   Solution = the most challenging of all scenarios: it would either require modifying the existing process if possible, or if the modification is not possible, then it would have to be replaced by a new process.

People often respect you for your expertise in some field. How have you been the expert?

An expert by definition is completely knowledgeable and experienced in a particular area. In this vast universe it is impossible to be an expert, as the knowledge that I have gained is only because I have been exposed to some aspects that are pertinent to an area of personal interest or aspects related to the field of work that I'm in. It is impossible to be completely knowledgeable on any particular aspect. I do not see myself as being an expert; however, others around me may see me as one.

You can stay absolutely focused and uninterrupted when necessary. Please give an example of this.

I've always been overweight, going right back to my school days. I reached a point where I had to address being overweight, so I decided to join a slimming clinic, knowing and understanding that I would have to adhere to a strict eating plan and give up eating all the foods that I currently enjoy. I joined the clinic and I started losing weight by following the strict eating plan that was created to me. Special meals were prepared for me. During this time the rest of the family enjoyed their meals that they always had. I kept focus on my objective to lose weight. There had been many opportunities for me cheat on the eating plan, but for the duration of the diet I abstained from eating anything other than what was on the eating plan.

At the end of the eight-month exercise I lost a total of 30 kg. This is only because I did not allow myself to be distracted from reaching my objective.

Your ability to analyse things in detail may sometimes frustrate others. How do you defend this need?

I usually say that 'the devil is in the detail' and it could ultimately result in the objective not being met in the desired time frame or the desired result could not be reached by the deadline. Ultimately it has to do with me being prepared. If there are several unknowns, then there is a difficulty in assessing the situation. By analysing things I'm better prepared and equipped to deal with a situation. If I don't analyse then I'm unprepared and any decision made at that point can be disastrous, as I have not had an opportunity to work through and digest all the information. I feel very uneasy and uncertain of how to react in that situation.

Observations of Type Five – the Investigator

- This Type Five was able to demonstrate the clear logic he uses in the intensity of studying the positions of taps. In problem-solving he has devised a statistical theory and he is clearly enthused in his quest to understand technology.
- His description of the disciplinary hearing was completely devoid of any emotional issues, although these procedures usually involve an employee being deeply affected in some way.
- Type Fives do not want to be put on the spot to make decisions. This Type Five clearly explains how he needs quiet time alone to mull things over in his head. He even chooses to do this when socialising to avoid the need for small talk.
- Although others might view him as an expert in certain fields, he believes this is not possible as knowledge is infinite and therefore he cannot be an expert.

Trigger points to becoming self-aware of your blind spots

- Conserving your energy – or being stingy. Remind yourself that there will be enough to go around, whether it is material things, your own time, resources or your emotions. The universe will provide.
- Believing that you are the expert on a subject. Remember that you might be in the know on certain topics but this does not give you the right to make others feel stupid because of your superior insight. Everyone can make a contribution.
- Being emotionally unavailable to others. It might not be easy for you to express your feelings to your nearest and dearest, but find other ways of showing your love through actions of kindness.
- Find a physical outlet which will make you feel you are using your energy in a way that does not only rely on your mental capacity.

How we can bring out the best in Type Fives

- They need space – this means they do not want to be crowded and require freedom to be alone to sort out their thoughts.
- Having too many social engagements will tire them out as they are happier in their own company or with their close family or friends.
- Give them the facts clearly when there is conflict. They will become confused if the situation is clouded with emotion and might resort to anger as a way to defend themselves.

- Lighten up – Type Fives have a quirky sense of humour and will delight you with their sense of the ridiculous.

- Do not be overdependent on a Type Five – they can be kind and helpful but will run a mile if they think someone is trying to emotionally manipulate a situation.

If Type Fives have experienced severe trauma in life they may develop schizotypal personality disorder (*DSM-IV*). This is characterised by eccentricities of thought and behaviour, but without clearly psychotic features.

At the highest level of development, Type Fives become profoundly focused in life in all the richness of opportunities – physically, emotionally and mentally.

CHAPTER ELEVEN

Type Six – the Loyalist

THE CHOSEN ANIMAL THAT SYMBOLISES THE TYPE SIX is the 'bokkie' or buck. It is skittish and will dart away at the slightest hint of threat. It also stays together in herds for life.

Others often see you as being reliable. In what way do people depend on you?

I have definitely experienced this and it allows people to come back to me again and again to assist them. People have commented that the work I do is well researched, comprehensive and correct.

Being organised in your life is important. What are the practical examples of this?

Especially in my work environment the standing joke is around the emphasis I place on scheduling. I want a schedule for everything. As long as I know a schedule has been compiled for a specific project, I am happy. It gives me the security that the product had been conceptualised, the timelines estimated and the completion date envisaged. As a manager all that is left to me is to ensure that the schedule and standards are adhered to.

There are times when you have difficulty making decisions. What are examples of when it has been hard to do this?

Unless I am convinced about the correctness of a decision, I prefer to have decisions made on my behalf. In the work environment where few decisions have a clear-cut answer, it creates stress for me as I always feel I cannot complete the investigative process before a decision needs to be made.

You can get caught up in worrying about what can go wrong in relationships or projects. How do you experience this?

I always track projects as I hope to catch the fallout before it happens. Mostly I 'waste' my time as my focus forces others to make sure the fallout does not happen. Or perhaps I worried unnecessarily!

You are typically cautious about committing to new relationships or ideas. What are the examples of this?

I think the way I make friends is an example. It would take me a very long time to call someone my friend and I am usually shocked when they start introducing me to others as their 'friend'.

Your true friendships often go back many years. What has been your experience of this?

I seem to have had only one real friend at a time. I somehow click with someone and then I treasure the relationship. I recall it was very difficult for me when I met my now husband. Forming that liaison really jeopardised my relationship with my 'girl' friend. Luckily, despite, or probably because, it had been a long-distance relationship, our friendship revived and lasted for more than 20 years now. Furthermore, I dated my husband for five years and we have been married for almost 12 years now. I am very loyal to my husband and will forgive a lot in order for our relationship to last.

When things go wrong you may be inclined to blame others or you can be harsh on yourself. How has this shown up for you?

I usually don't blame others, but would rather say I will take the punch. I find that others stand amazed by this attitude of mine.

Sometimes you see the glass as half empty rather than half full. What are examples of this?

Now this is a reality check! My husband often will say that I see the glass half empty. And usually I am taken aback as I am stating the 'reality'.

Others really do need to prove themselves before you will trust them. In what circumstance has this been so?

Especially in the work environment it happens regularly. I, as the manager, would appoint people and only if they prove themselves would I allow them to work independently. I play the role of tutor and micromanager to ensure this happening.

You usually have a 'plan B' in case things go wrong. What examples are there of this being the case?

I mostly do not have a plan B as my support structure in the past did not allow me the freedom. I have adapted by comprehensively planning an almost foolproof plan A. I do, however, still feel the stresses of not having a plan B, C or D.

Observations of Type Six – the Loyalist

- This Type Six acknowledges that people find her completely reliable due to her outputs being well researched, comprehensive and correct.
- She recognises that scheduling gives her security. This is also demonstrated in her not seeing the need for 'plan B' – her plan A already contains a plan A, B, C and D. She teases herself for her tendency to worry, but again relies on the plan for no fallout.
- Doubt can cause her stress and she prefers to defer decisions to others if they are too difficult. She is happy to consider the half-empty glass as reality.
- Her friendships are grown from trust, and loyalty is implicit in her relationships. She is shocked when acquaintances call the relationship a 'friendship'.

Trigger points to becoming self-aware of your blind spots

- When you feel anxious about things, think back on how you have in the past worried needlessly about calamities which never materialised.
- Learn to trust your own judgement. Having a wise sounding board is great, but you do not need to get advice from others every time you make a decision.
- When you feel stressed by life situations, be careful of projecting your negative thoughts onto others. You might regret mean utterances which were not fair or deserved by another.
- You take your commitments in life very seriously. Sometimes you can be unnecessarily harsh on yourself. Take time out to enjoy life and graciously accept time out when it is offered to you.
- Be aware of sabotaging your own success because you might be doubting yourself. Stand back and be objective about your accomplishments and gift in life.

How to bring out the best in Type Sixes

Appreciate their loyalty and do not give them cause to distrust you by being unreliable or insincere.

When they are being 'testy', support them with genuine reassurance to ease their anxiety rather than trying to win the argument.

Do not be offended when they do not act on your advice after they have asked for it. They will probably have sought advice from various sources and might in the end decide on a completely different plan of action.

Humour will help them to lighten up and they can often see the ridiculous things in life. Enjoy a good chuckle with them or invite them out for a fun activity.

When they stress over what might go wrong, rather appreciate their ability to foresee life's potential mishaps in having thought of 'plan B'.

Type Sixes have experienced some severe trauma in life they may develop paranoid personality disorder (*DSM-IV*). This is characterised by suspicion of others' motives, but not to the point of delusion.

At the highest level of development Type Sixes are enabled to honour authority and are trusting of themselves and others.

CHAPTER TWELVE

Type Seven – the Enthusiast

THE CHOSEN CREATURE FOR THE TYPE SEVEN is the colourful butterfly
flits from one flower to another, seldom staying put for long.

You are known to be spontaneous in your response to life stimulus. Descr
a situation typical of this.
I was unexpectedly offered an opportunity to relocate from South Africa to
UK to work for the Walt Disney Company. Six days later, after hasty consultat
with family, I accepted the position, and three months later the family
uprooted and embarked on an adventure that would involve a similar relocat
to France three years later. It is a matter of jumping at opportunities that a
and seeing the potential in them.

You enjoy adventure and love to explore new things. Tell us about s
a story.
I had an aunt living in an old *mulino* in Tuscany, Italy, whom I had never visi
As I was going to the Bologna book fair I thought I'd take off a week on my c
and visit her and see the sights. Unfortunately she had no phone and the c
way of contacting her was by letter. I duly wrote to her and gave her the d
but due to time constraints never received a reply. Armed with only her phy:
address and map in hand, on arrival at the airport I boarded a train, the
coach, then a taxi and was ferried to San Donato. After 20 hours in transit
after traipsing the area I discovered that there are several San Donatos in
and I'd arrived at the wrong one. It happened to be Good Friday, and taxis
public transport had stopped running so there was no possibility of loca
her and I was stranded.
     The nearest town that offered accommodation was the beautiful medi
walled city of San Gimignano which was the centre of Easter celebrations
inundated with tourists. I spent a further four hours wheeling my suitcas

d down steep cobbled streets in search of accommodation with no luck and
s seriously considering a police cell as an attractive alternative when I saw a
rman tourist letting himself into a *penzione*. I accosted him and asked if he
uld beg the landlady to make an extra place, which she eventually agreed to.
pent the night in her son's room out of which I was unceremoniously ejected
to a sofa in the passage when he arrived home unexpectedly. The following
y I rather amazingly managed to locate my aunt on the other side of Tuscany.
hen I arrived she had just received my letter and was wondering how on earth
ould ever find her.

ere are times when you become scattered and you may even lose things.
hat brings this on? Please give an example.
hen I go supermarket shopping my husband refuses to go with me as I can
re at a shelf mesmerised for several seconds and forget what I'm looking
. Because I want to try everything, too much choice seems to flummox me.
ariably I leave with loads of interesting items, forgetting the essentials I went
get. I also become scattered in thinking about a problem and get side-tracked
o all sorts of related and often peripheral issues.

u can hold opinions firmly and may even be considered to be superior at
nes. How do you relate to this?
now that this can be true of me but I have learned to be much more
ommodating of other people's opinions, which is not always easy. Sometimes
ople interpret my being opinionated as arrogance, particularly outside of the
rking environment.

redom is hard for you to deal with. How and when do you typically
perience this?
ake sure that I never have the chance to get bored. I fill up my life with so
ny activities that it is not possible to have time for boredom. The only times
t bored it is usually in a group environment such as a lecture theatre where I
e no control over the proceedings and I don't find the information useful or
ue adding but I am compelled to remain. Then I start fidgeting and can work
self up into quite a state of anger over the time wasted.

When things become too painful you may find an escape. Can you recount example of this happening?

Years ago after an altercation with my first husband, I spontaneously fou a tent and sleeping bag, got in the car, and drove to Hermanus, checked ir a campsite for the weekend and had a marvellous time painting and doi ceramics on my own.

Your lust for life may bring about over-indulgence in some way. How do y experience this?

Oh dear. Buffets. Don't let me near a buffet or one of those 'eat all you c restaurants. I absolutely love my food and it is a serious vice. If we go t Chinese restaurant or somewhere where they serve *mezze* platters, I always f that I'm going to miss out so I order five separate dishes instead of the usual t or three. At a recent breakfast event I ate my breakfast and then proceeded consume the spare one due to our HR manager who didn't want it and I insis they bring it for me… If I'm on a plane and they've got a spare meal going, ask for it – so I can have the chicken AND the beef.

You are known to see the sunny side of things, especially in the face difficulty. Can you tell us about a time when this was the case?

I'm definitely the eternal optimist and I like to believe the best of peopl recently organised my husband's 50th birthday party to coincide with housewarming of our newly built holiday house. We had friends with sn children arriving from France the morning of the party. A week before event, my husband visited the house and said it was nowhere nearly ready we should cancel the party. He was in a real panic as no balustrades had go up yet, the toilets weren't connected and the kitchen hadn't been installed. I s it would all be fine and 'not to worry'. We scraped in just in time. On the ni people arrived the holes for the balustrades were still being drilled.

Meeting new people and expressing yourself with ease has always co naturally for you. Can you describe this?

I love to meet new people as they always offer some new perspective on What is there to be afraid of?

u have an appetite for experiencing new places, people and experiences.
ow have you found an outlet for this?

ave travelled widely in my employment for which I am very grateful and I
get itchy feet if I'm in one place for too long without stimulation. Reindeer
dging in Lapland, getting caught in a snow storm in South Korea and bargain
nting in Beijing are some highlights. I tend not to go to the same restaurants
er and over but try to experience something different. When travelling I will
o try and eat different and unfamiliar food types (only once if necessary) and
rticularly to try local cuisine.

bservations of a Type Seven – the Enthusiast

This Type Seven gives rich descriptions of her lust for life and travel.
Moving from one job to another in the same town is a big deal for most
people but she revelled in the adventure of moving jobs from one country
to another.
Type Sevens are very optimistic and this is well demonstrated in her
arriving in Tuscany to visit an aunt with no address or firm arrangements.
However, this provided another exciting romp of adventure for the lively
Type Seven. Planning and 'can do' also feature high for Type sevens as
described in getting their holiday home ready for her husband's birthday
party.
Dealing with painful events is problematic for Type Sevens and they will
usually find a way to avoid the messiness of life. This Type Seven went on a
camping adventure when faced with the pain of an ending relationship.
Boredom does not feature in a Type Seven's life and this is demonstrated
by how she only experiences boredom when others are in control, such as
being a participant in a lecture.

gger points to becoming self-aware of your blind spots

Notice when you become overenthusiastic and take over the 'air time' by
not listening to others and possibly shutting them down.
When you are confronted by a painful situation, don't just block it out. Stay
with the sensation, talk it over with a trusted person and then move on
when you have truly dealt with the situation.
Recognise your lust for life. Rather than overindulging, slow down and
appreciate the small and simple things which nature offers you.
Be aware of not becoming too excited by situations. Your natural pendulum

will swing back and you may find yourself feeling down by the same quantum.

- Spend some time thinking about the consequences of your plans. There is usually a downside to most things and just being aware will equip you to handle the inevitable pebbles in your pathway.

How we can bring out the best in Type Sevens

- Even though they sound very confident about their plans, be careful about giving them feedback. Listen to them until they have exhausted the topic, then state your case factually and with conviction.
- Encourage them to talk about what really matters but respect that they find it very hard to talk about their emotional pain.
- Type Sevens need freedom to explore their adventures. If you give them unconditional love they will reciprocate.
- Share fun times, laughter and their genuine appreciation for life.
- Be brief and focused in your story as they become bored with too much detail.

If Type Sevens have experienced some severe trauma in life they may develop bipolar disorder which is characterised by manic episodes alternating with major depressive episodes.

At the highest level of development Type Sevens become deeply grateful even the simple and understated things that life has to offer.

In the following chapter we will consider some of the finer, complex aspects the Enneagram.

CHAPTER THIRTEEN

Other interesting aspects of the Enneagram

THE THREE CENTRES OR TRIADS

Identifying a person's Centre is an important indicator of his or her true Enneagram type. The three Centres or Triads demonstrate that Types Eight, Nine and One form the Instinctive (or Moving) Centre; Types Two, Three and Four form the Feeling Centre; and Types Five, Six and Seven form the Thinking Centre. The Centres can be likened to the innate intelligence of human beings – the components of essence and roughly correspond to the Eastern concept of chakras. *Chakra* is the Sanskrit word for the seven main vortices of energy in the human being.

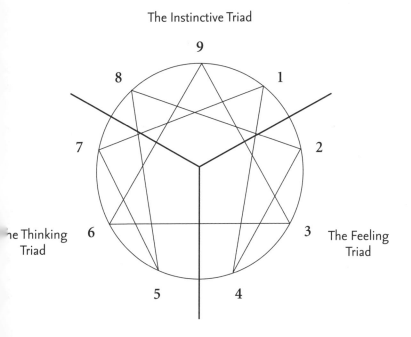

The Instinctive Triad

The Thinking Triad

The Feeling Triad

The personality is based upon, and people's psychological problems ar:
from, imbalances between the thinking, feeling and instinctive Centres. Nich
(1985) describes the Triads as shown below.

The Thinking Centre (Types Five, Six and Seven)

This Centre controls the thinking and intellectual functions. The following ;
capacities to the Thinking Centre: repetition of words and phrases, mechani
talking, inquisitiveness, shrewdness, desire to know and understand, sear
for knowledge, higher levels of imagination, intellectual construction, creat
thought and discovery. Negative descriptors include negativity, fault findi:
disagreeing, nitpicking, hair splitting, criticising and disparaging.

The Feeling Centre (Types Two, Three and Four)

This Centre is concerned with the expression of emotional energy, with attracti
and repulsion, like and dislike. The following are capacities to the Emotio
Centre: mechanical expression of emotions, all emotions relating to one's li:
and dislikes, personal emotions, daily 'wills', small desires, religious and aesthe
emotions, moral feelings, artistic creation, the beginnings of conscience.

The Moving or Instinctive Centre (Types Eight, Nine and One)

The Moving Centre controls what might be referred to as the intelligence
the body. This deals with the 'animal' knowledge, instincts, and coordinat:
and survival skills of the organism. The following are capacities to the Mov
Centre: automatic reflexes, imitation on a small scale, limited adaptability
learning new movements of the body, pleasure in movement, enjoyment
games, some forms of acting, inventing and making adaptations of things.

The Moving or Instinctive Centre is also referred to as the Belly Centre
Kath, a name from Eastern esoteric tradition. The Japanese call it the *hara* and
Chinese *tan-t'ien*. It is the Centre of the inner physiology and refers to the pers
sense of grounding, of being solidly on the feet, embodied and in the world.

The wings

In the Enneagram model no person is a pure personality type: everyone
unique mixture of his or her basic type and usually one of the two types adjac
to it on the circumference of the Enneagram. One of the two types adjacent to
basic type is called the 'wing'. There is disagreement among the various traditi
of the Enneagram about whether individuals have one or two wings.

This can be illustrated as follows: If a Type Nine has a Type One wing he or
e is more likely to be more critical and self-disciplined. A Type Nine with a
pe Eight wing is more likely to demonstrate flashes of anger and overall will
more easygoing than the Type Nine with the Type One wing.

It is useful to study the types on either side of the type which you believe to
your dominant type. You can then decide which is likely to be your wing.

ints of integration and disintegration

e way the numbered points are connected, as illustrated on the next page, is
nificant because the lines connect the real type to two other types in either
ealthy or unhealthy way. Some Enneagram teachers and researchers believe
t people integrate to one of the types and disintegrate from another type.
wever, I have found from personal observation that people take on both
althy or unhealthy aspects of the connecting types.

It is therefore important that once you have recognised your true type, you
o familiarise yourself with the blind spots and gifts of both your connecting
es. This will give you more insight to your personality and behaviours.

I have left the arrows in the diagram as you may in fact find that you do
egrate or disintegrate in the way the arrows indicate. Some teachers believe
t we integrate along the arrow of positive direction as an act of will to
w up as more honest and present. This means we don't forget our negative
t stories but rather that we choose to forgive past hurts and take complete
ponsibility for our actions in the moment.

I observed that people may demonstrate behaviours from the points of
egration and disintegration. A person who identifies with Type Three and
ght be stressed or lacking in self-awareness might take on the unhealthy qualities
Type Six and become distrustful and paranoid, even taking on the unhealthy
lities of Type Nine and becoming lazy and disconnected from others.

Similarly, someone who identifies with Type Three but is operating at a
lthy and self-aware level may take on the healthy levels of Type Six – being
npassionate and caring about colleagues – and the healthy level of Type Nine,
being both serene and involved in the organisation. I am of the opinion that
en people are more self-aware and less stressed, they are also able to cope
h conflict in a more effective way.

The arrows in the following figures indicate the directions of integration and
ntegration for each type.

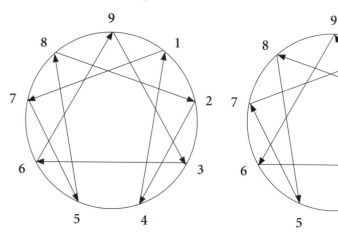

Direction of integration

Direction of disintegration

Levels of development

Riso and Hudson have been praised for their key contribution to t
Enneagram, namely the development of a highly sophisticated map of
levels of psychological development for each personality type, from the m
pathological to the healthiest.

Most people living average lives, who are gainfully employed, are operati
from the average levels of personality. People who are more deeply self-aw
are more likely to be operating at the healthy levels and those who are dee
distressed will operate from the unhealthy levels. It is important to n
that people can easily move quite dramatically either up or down the lev
depending on their personality, stability or life stresses and shocks.

The levels of development as identified by Hudson and Riso support
research by Daniel Goleman (1999) on emotional intelligence. People w
higher self-awareness operate at the higher levels of their Enneagram ty
Unresolved childhood issues, stress factors at work or home, and dysfunctio
work situations are all factors that could influence the levels at which individu
might operate at any given time.

The clear descriptions of the levels for each Enneagram type are useful
that they offer a clear insight for the coach or teacher and the individual into
levels of emotional intelligence at which the individual is operating. Althou
circumstances can influence people to lower these levels, I believe that the m
stable the person is and the more practised in self-awareness, the more likel
is that he or she will deal with the external factors.

A difficulty with the levels is that of course there is no way to accurately ;ess where we are in the levels. The other complexity is that no matter how tegrated or healthy our personalities, we can still 'lose it' and move way down ese levels when we are really stressed by life situations. Likewise we may have)ments of absolute clarity and compassion and have perspectives right from : top of the level of integration.

e instinctual subtypes

e personality can also be viewed in terms of subtypes, which are 'self-:servation', 'social' and 'sexual'. These are not subsets of Enneagram Types, but her *instincts* stemming from our animal evolution. The term 'sexual' is often sunderstood. It does not refer to the sexual act, but rather to an intensity of imacy. Each of the Enneagram types has a stacking of subtypes: the most minant, a second subtype and a third subtype. The subtypes are referred to as tinctual' because people have no choice over the way in which the subtypes stacked, but with self-awareness people can learn ways to balance their ptypes. Helen Palmer refers to these instincts as Subtypes and Riso-Hudson r to them as Instinctual Variants.

The 'self-preservation' subtype is focused on matters of survival, comfort, lth, security and the accumulation of resources; the 'social' subtype, is focused relationships and interactions among the group; and the 'sexual' subtype, is used on matters of intimacy and bonding with significant others.

)ne of these instinctual drives is dominant in each person, and his or her ds and values tend to cluster around it. People who share a particular sonality type will show distinct differences based on their own subtype. For mple, a social Type Three will be much more status- and image-conscious n a self-preserving Type Three, who will be focused more overtly on duction than image.

Ve need all three of the instincts to survive in the world, but the order of the king differs from person to person. The last instinct in the stacking is the which we usually neglect. My stacking is: Sexual (dominant), then Social lastly Self-Preservation. I have needed to pay attention to the neglected inct of Self-Preservation in ensuring that I eat healthily, that I manage my : and that I am aware of security risks. My husband's stacking is Sexual ninant) – this has made for a very happy and lasting relationship! – and Self-Preservation and Social is the neglected instinct. He takes care of the ily finances and is the resident chef. But I am concerned with our social life in inviting friends and family to our home to enjoy the crayfish he catches a the dinners he prepares.

Sikora's model, as illustrated in the following table, has useful applicati in a work context, because it suggests the strengths and weaknesses of t subtypes. I have found this to be an insightful approach in coaching peo¡ who are confused about their career choices.

Instinctual variants (subtypes) at work – subtype strengths and weaknesses

DOMINANT INSTINCT (SUBTYPE)	IS NATURALLY DRAWN TO	MAY NEGLECT
Self-preservation	The Nuts and Bolts – administrative issues; structures, processes and procedures; playing the devil's advocate; finances and budgeting; organisation of tools and materials	The Sizzle – presentation/promotion of self and product; networking with and charming others; competition
Sexual	The Sizzle – presentation/promotion of self and product; networking with and charming others; competition	The Culture Group – dynamics; interpersonal communication; social cohesion and mores
Social	The Culture Group – dynamics; interpersonal communication; social cohesion and mores	The Nuts and Bolts – administrative issues; structures, processes and procedures; playing the devil's advocate; finances and budgeting; organisation of tools and materials

Source: *Sikora (2006)*

ne table below illustrates the leadership strengths and weaknesses of the
btypes.

ubtype and leadership strengths and weaknesses

OMINANT INSTINCT UBTYPE)	TYPICAL LEADERSHIP STRENGTHS	POTENTIAL LEADERSHIP WEAKNESSES
elf-preservation	Administration and processing data; predicting problems; creating processes; sober and dependable; effective in budget and finance issues	May be too introverted; focus on task rather than interpersonal issues; lack of charisma; cautious rather than risk-taking; detached rather than inspirational
exual	Generally more charismatic and dynamic than the other subtypes; good at building relationships with customers, channel partners and strategic allies; good at selling both inside and outside the organisation; inspiring the workforce towards daunting goals	May be too focused on charisma and neglect shaping the organisation's culture; can neglect career development of subordinates; self-focus may lead to putting own interests ahead of the good of the company and employees
cial	Understanding interpersonal dynamics and organisational culture; building teams; building consensus and shaping group identity; big-picture, strategic thinking	May fail to pay attention to administrative details and neglect processes and procedures; may struggle with making difficult personnel decisions such as firing or reprimanding underperformers

ce: *Sikora (2006)*

The Hornevian Triad

This triad consists of the Compliant (Types One, Two and Six), Assertive (Type Three, Seven and Eight) and Withdrawn (Types Four, Five and Nine) styles. Ri and Hudson (1999) have named these three groups the Hornevian Groups social styles, in honour of Karen Horney. Horney was a revolutionary psycholog who in the 1940s identified a list of 10 needs that people present with which turn may be grouped into these three major adjustment patterns. Each of t three patterns describes the person's adjustment to other people:

- **Moving towards people (Compliant): Types One, Two and Six**
  This adjustment pattern includes the person's need for affection and approval, for a dominant partner to control a person's life, and to live life within narrow limits. In sum this person needs to be liked, wanted, desire loved; to feel accepted, welcomed, approved of or appreciated; to be need to be of importance to others, especially to one particular person; and to be helped, protected, taken care of and guided. These people see themselv as unselfish and self-sacrificing individuals who deserve to be loved unconditionally and are therefore able to mask their extreme dependency They are essentially the Compliant type.

- **Moving against people (Assertive): Types Three, Seven and Eight**
  In most ways, these people are the opposite of the Compliant type. This does not suggest that they are likely to break all the rules in the book, but rather that they find it easy to reject others' opinions and will easily confront others without fear of rejection. This adjustment pattern combines a person's needs for power, exploitation of others, and personal prestige and achievement. Such people will assess any situation or relationship from the standpoint of *What can I get out of it?* This may apply to money, prestige, contacts or ideas. These people see themselves as powerful, respected leaders and are able to disguise any feelings of dependence, which they cannot acknowledge.

- **Moving away from people (Withdrawn): Types Four, Five and Nine**
  This adjustment pattern includes the needs for self-sufficiency, independence, perfection and unassailability. What is crucial is the individuals' need to put emotional distance between themselves and oth They draw themselves a kind of magic circle that no one may penetrate. They seem to be saying: 'If I withdraw, nothing can hurt me.' Withdrawn aloof types of people suppress their need for affection by seeing themsel as self-sufficient and independent, needing nothing from anyone.

The Hornevian social styles

ASSERTIVE STYLE	COMPLIANT STYLE	WITHDRAWN STYLE
Enneagram Types Three, Seven and Eight	Enneagram Types One, Two and Six	Enneagram Types Four, Five and Nine
Moving against people	Moving towards people	Moving away from people
Ego-oriented and ego expansive	Share a need to be of service to others	Unconscious often wells up through daydreams and fantasies
Respond to stress by building up, reinforcing	Respond to stress by consulting 'superego' to find right thing to do	Respond to stress by moving away from the world into their imagination
Difficulty in processing feelings	Try to obey internalised rules from childhood	Difficulty moving from imagination to action
Type Threes are aggressive in pursuit of their goals and in their competition with others	Type Ones are compliant to the ideals after which they strive	Type Fours are withdrawn to protect their feelings and their fragile self-image
Type Sevens are aggressive about engaging the environment and satisfying their appetites	Type Twos are compliant to the superego's direction to be always selfless and loving	Type Fives are withdrawn, away from action, into their thoughts
Type Eights are aggressive about asserting themselves against others and the environment	Type Sixes are compliant to the superego's direction to do what is expected of them	Type Nines are withdrawn so that others will not disturb their inner peacefulness
Insist on/demand what they want	Earn things by placating the superego	Withdraw to get what they want
Approach is active and direct	Try to be good boys and girls	Disengage from others to deal with their needs

Source: *Riso & Hudson (1999)*

CHAPTER FOURTEEN

The Enneagram as a tool fo dealing with conflict

Causes of conflict situations

People cannot always control of their psychological and physical heal although they can take responsibility for making life choices that will promc good health. Illness, whether temporary or permanent, can affect the way peoj deal with conflict. The degree of empathy that people can show each other ai influences how conflict is dealt with. Some Enneagram types are more eas disposed to empathy than others.

Stress is a further factor affecting the way people deal with conflict; soi individuals have better stress-coping mechanisms than others. Childho experiences, too, have a major influence on how people handle conflict. Parer peers and teachers influence children; and similarly, the culture informs peop responses to conflict, since some cultures are more robust and others m diplomatic in the way people engage with each other.

People are subjected to reports of violence and conflict every day throu the media or even through personal experience. The more horrific the stor the better the newspapers sell. People often then 'zone out' in front of tl television sets at night, only to be further subjected to emotional drama a violence. Many individuals have abandoned religion, and children are be brought up with shaky value systems. These circumstances are not conduc to the development of creative mindsets and a willingness to foster heal working relationships.

Children growing up in South Africa are confronted with many so challenges no matter which demographic strata or economic levels they mi come from. It could also be argued that the present-day generation suf from many psychological issues that have remained unresolved because of follies of previous generations, which may affect the way in which they sl up at work and parent their own children. Most people accept that they do have the power or capacity to change others, therefore any person faced wi

tuation of conflict needs to rely on his or her own internal resources to resolve
onflict. Furthermore, conflict is often hidden, or 'subliminal', liable to give rise
to what may be termed 'unconscious' conflict situations.

ffects of conflict

dividual, dysfunctional conflicts result in damage to physical and emotional
ellbeing, and loss of confidence and self-esteem. At a psychological level,
ommon reactions include an inability to concentrate and think clearly, with
n increase in irritability and an inability to relax. Minor physical ailments such
headaches, difficulty in sleeping and upset stomachs are also warning signs
at, if left unheeded, may lead to ulcers and high blood pressure. Behavioural
gns may involve withdrawal from relationships that are proving difficult, in
dition to the overuse of alcohol, cigarettes or tranquillisers in an attempt
relieve tension. There is often a vicious cycle: conflicts lead to stress, which
turn results in an increase in cynicism about clients, colleagues, family and
ends, which leads to further conflict. Managing interpersonal conflicts is
erefore an important contributor to the reduction of stress in our lives.
Many situations of negative conflict can be avoided if people do not take
ings personally. If you make a habit of not taking anything personally you
n't need to place your trust in what others say or do. You will only need to
st yourself to make responsible choices. You are never responsible for the
ions of others; you are only responsible for you. When you truly understand
s, and refuse to take things personally, you can hardly be hurt by the careless
mments or actions of others.

nflict descriptors

e Enneagram is a robust model which can assist people in any sphere of
to 'look into the mirror' to develop their own individual personal growth
l self-awareness. When people begin to understand the motivations for their
aviour, and especially the reasons for dysfunctional conflict situations, they
decide to adopt different behaviours.
Palmer and Sikora have ascribed conflict descriptors to each Enneagram
e, as described below. This research is useful for people who wish to grow
their self-awareness, as it helps show them that they might be reacting to
flict situations in automatic or reactive ways. Similarly, they may use this
wledge in order to gain a better understanding of where their 'opponents'
likely to be positioned when conflict arises.

	PALMER'S DESCRIPTORS	SIKORA'S DESCRIPTORS
Type Ones	Feel secure with guidelines and strict accountability	Able to leave emotions aside – logical and dispassionate
	May feel controlled and stifled by demands for meetings and reports	If self-aware, do not take disputes personally
	Like to make binding rules	See things in black and white
	May limit others' options and ambitions	Logic may be more geared to making their point than listening to others
	Peer conflict typically focuses on their need to be right: 'It wasn't my fault'	Can become rigid and entrenched in own point of view
	Refuse to pick up others' responsibility	As stress increases, may become strident or shut down
Type Twos	Can be temperamental	Strive to resolve disputes though cooperation
	Irritable with and dismissive of implied disrespect	Can be pushovers
	Pride will not allow them to be kept waiting and will not countenance the mundane	Once in conflict may become assertive
	Become angry if overlooked	Good at resolving third-party conflicts
	Personal problems may leak into workplace	May resist compromise and can become vocal
	Disappear when confronted by big emotions	May become accusing of others
	Not only forgive, they forget	If highly stressed, become aggressive and volatile
Type Threes	Expect everyone to be task- and role-oriented	Can resolve conflict unemotionally

	PALMER'S DESCRIPTORS	SIKORA'S DESCRIPTORS
	Furious when projects are interrupted	May view conflict resolution as a waste of time
	When trouble arises, impatience is evident in conversation	View conflict as an impediment to getting things done
	With bad news, first reaffirms the positive	Focus more on winning than compromise
	Power struggles may arise between them and others	Can become combative, arrogant and evasive
	Need to be reassured that goal is still possible	May go behind people's backs to garner support from influential people
Type Fours	Can make others feel deficient	If self-aware, can use empathy and insight to resolve disputes
	Adopt a push-pull style of relating	Shyness can prevent them from being open
	Avoid the known, wanting to follow new and more exciting routes	The need to process thoughts and feelings leads to hesitation
	Can be biting towards immediate competitors	May appear aloof and stubborn
	Insist that colleagues choose sides	May retreat and sulk, unwilling to listen
Type Fives	Not available to others	Detached and unemotional when faced with conflict
	Lack of opposition can be confused with support	Uncomfortable with others' emotions during conflict
	Others are not aware of their decision-making processes	Others may feel frustrated at their lack of emotion
	Can make decisions without apparent input from others	Tend to flee from conflict

	PALMER'S DESCRIPTORS	SIKORA'S DESCRIPTORS
	Few defences against public confrontation	May appear arrogant, uninterested and unwilling to engage others
	Others may perceive them as callous and high-handed	If self-aware, can see where things went wrong
Type Sixes	A rush of enthusiasm makes them cautious	May overreact to conflict, becoming fearful and aggressive
	May be perceived as negative	See relatively minor conflict as threatening
	Anti-authoritarianism is a potential conflict area	Want alignment with the group – may see disagreement as being attacked
	Need non-threatening people on their team	Unaware of growth potential of conflict
	Success gives them confidence	Tend to stereotype
Type Sevens	May seek shortcuts to avoid pain	If self-aware, can handle conflict well by focusing on positives
	Desire to equalise authority can create conflicts	Generally avoid conflict as it is unpleasant
	Tend to avoid conflict and to avert criticisms	Usually retreat first, then become demanding
	Exaggerated, promissory plans may terminate in poor follow-through	If everyone can focus on an exciting future, problems will go away
	Avoid nitty-gritty detail	May find it hard to focus on the other person's story
	Can be guilty of not sharing the load	Dismiss others' grievances with their bad behaviour

	PALMER'S DESCRIPTORS	SIKORA'S DESCRIPTORS
Type Eights	Must take action when they feel threatened	Enjoy some degree of conflict
	Often perceived as troublemakers	Fighting a cause or opponent is energising
	Can be seen as aggressive complainers	State their agenda but do not listen to others
	Push the limits for clarity	Tend to make demands rather than requests
	Fight to win	Often act too quickly, without considering others' feelings
	Can go over heads and manipulate	When bored can go looking for a fight
	Compromise feels like capitulation	See life as a battlefield with enemies everywhere
	Mediation is for wimps	Try to resolve conflict by force
Type Nines	Start off as ambivalent and then turn to stubborn non-communication	Work hard to avoid conflict
	Whoever gets their ear gets heard	Enjoy arguments about politics, sport, religion, etc.
	Inadvertently create conflict by withholding information	Good mediators for third-party conflict
	Their 'non action' strategy can infuriate others	Naturally supportive and ensure that both sides are heard and appreciated
	Passive-aggressive – 'Will only do as much as I'm paid for'	Have difficulty setting boundaries and may become overwhelmed
	When stubborn, can be selfish and uncompromising	Can show bursts of anger as stress increases

Source: Palmer (1988); Sikora (2006)

Identify your style of conflict

CONFLICT ASSESSMENT QUESTIONNAIRE

When answering these questions, picture yourself in a real-life situation whe[re] you experienced some conflict with another. Place a cross next to the o[ne] statement which best describes you for each number, i.e. a, b or c.

Remember to do this test in pencil or on another piece of paper so that othe[rs] may also use the questionnaire.

1.
- a │ I usually avoid taking a position that would create controversy
- b │ I try to show the logic and benefits of my position
- c │ I am usually firm in pursuing my goals

2.
- a │ I usually lean to a direct discussion of the problem
- b │ I attempt to get all the facts and issues out in the open
- c │ I sometimes allow others to solve the problem

3.
- a │ I will confront others if they are wrong or uninformed
- b │ If it makes the other person happy I will let them maintain their vie[w]
- c │ I will confront others if they are being unfair

4.
- a │ I avoid hurting others feelings
- b │ I try to do what is right to avoid useless tension
- c │ I am known to speak my mind

a   I react to difficulties immediately

b   I try to postpone issues to think them over

c   I will consider the appropriate course of action before responding

a   I will give away points as long as I'm allowed to have some too

b   I try to win my position

c   I will hold my tongue if it means others are not antagonised

a   I will push to get my point made and accepted

b   I try to do what is necessary to avoid tension

c   It is usually not worth worrying about differences of opinion

a   I might try to soothe others' feelings to preserve our relationship

b   I make sure I have the correct story before confronting others

c   I assert my wishes to achieve my goals

a   I go out of my way to meet my responsibilities to others

b   I won't back down if I'm in the right

c   I often sacrifice my wishes for the wishes of someone else

10. a | I sometimes have a sense of being different when meeting others

b | I need to be accepted for who I am

c | I am confident in approaching strangers

11. a | I value being able to contribute to helping others

b | It is important to get what one sets out to achieve in life

c | Not getting your own way is often less important than hurting oth

12. a | Having time out is a good way for me to meet my needs

b | I can handle being teased and will use humour to win others over

c | It troubles me when others have sloppy standards

13. a | Time for dreaming is rewarding in itself

b | If you don't insist on what you want, it doesn't happen

c | One should work hard to earn one's rewards

14. a | Those who push hardest usually get to the top

b | Being true to oneself is most important

c | Honouring our beliefs is what we should strive for

Place the same cross on the score sheet as you have on your answer sheet.

QUESTION	1	2	3	4	5	6	7	8	9	10	11	12	13	14	Total no. of crosses
ROW 1	C	a	a	c	a	b	a	c	b	c	b	b	b	a	
ROW 2	B	b	c	b	b	a	b	b	a	b	a	c	c	c	
ROW 3	A	c	b	a	c	c	c	a	c	a	c	a	a	b	
													Total		14

f you scored most crosses in Row 1 you are likely to be an Assertive Type.

f you scored most crosses in Row 2 you are most likely to be a Compliant Type.

f you scored most crosses in Row 3 you are most likely to be a Withdrawn Type.

The following observations were gathered from each of the three conflict types when I conducted conflict management workshops at my workplace.

Dealing with conflict as an Assertive Type – Typically includes Enneagram Types Three, Seven and Eight

Assertives readily admit that they often engage in aggression when faced with conflict. However, they warn others not to retaliate with aggression as this could escalate the conflict. They expressly want others to avoid bringing any emotion to bear, which they consider to be soppiness, but to rather stick to facts. They welcome others to express themselves 'straight'. Implicit in this request is that the 'facts' they demand are based on their own structure of interpretation and a disregard for the views of others. Others' viewpoints are often considered to be irrelevant or 'hogwash'.

They warn others not to raise their voice first, allowing them to take the lead in the race of raising voices. Raising their voice in conflict seems normal to them and they wish not to be questioned about this but rather for others to focus on the issue being discussed. Similarly, they warn others not to show threatening body language as they will retaliate. They acknowledge that they might 'lose it' at times and then would want others to give them time to cool down.

They demand that others should hear their full version before being interrupted. They are inviting of a heated debate as long as others do not attack them personally but rather focus on the topic being discussed. Assertives express a fear of being ignored, and want their ideas and suggestions to be acknowledged. They suggested that others should engage them by focusing on what is right rather than on what is wrong. They are willing to debate negatives, but choose to start off looking at the positives. They also want to avoid nitpicking and would rather look at the 'bigger picture' when discussing problems.

Although they prefer straight communication, they do not want others to decide matters for them and have an intense dislike of being judged harshly or controlled. They also need space around themselves. Assertives are aware that they might come across too boldly to others, and therefore ask others not be too sensitive when they become impassioned. They do not mean harm to their opponents but feel fiercely about the subject matter. They do not want others to withdraw from them, but rather to hear them out. They enjoy being challenged and eagerly wait to hear the others' argument. They prefer to hear bad news exactly as it is rather than hearing a softer, possibly less real, version. They also want to hear the news immediately.

Advice for Assertives

Assertives should be mindful that they can be perceived as too strong and pushy and may offend others rather than encourage the resolving of conflict. They should be willing to allow others to air their opinions and focus on active listening by being more patient. Their straight talking may be offensive to others and it is useful to use language that is more empathetic. Awareness of their voice will assist them in lowering it and not creating unnecessary tension. Allowing others to express their emotions may go a long way towards diffusing a conflict situation.

Dealing with conflict as a Compliant Type – typically includes Enneagram Types One, Two and Six

Compliants have a strong need to be listened to. They feel strongly that they do not want to be interrupted, and need time to tell their version of events and their interpretations. This suggests that others need to be patient with them even if they are inclined to be verbose in responding to situations of conflict.

They also express a need for others to deal with them in a sensitive way but also do not want others to confuse emotions with facts. Appreciation for empathy is acknowledged. Their request that others remain open minded suggests that they believe they themselves have the answers and are automatically in the right. In addition, their need for compromise indicates that others should accommodate their position towards *their* point of view. They also want to be acknowledged for their point of view and contribution to the discussion. Comments such as 'We mean well', and 'Don't withdraw from us' reveal a need to move towards others in situations of conflict. There is a high need for respect, principled debate, adherence to rules and factual references. Sensitivity to the perception that others might be patronising or pretentious in any way towards them is highlighted.

A common wish is that others should not bring up issues from the past, but should rather focus on the facts of the current debate. Being personally criticised is raised as being difficult for them to deal with. This resonates with their need to have others focus on facts and not feelings, as mentioned above. This group also expresses the desire that conflict be dealt with privately and not in a group environment. They are sensitive to voice tone and body language. Others should be mindful of not overpowering them. They express a need for conflict to be dealt with speedily and not to be buried or trivialised.

Advice for Compliants

Compliants should be willing to push back at Assertives and not be too quick to judge others. They could also 'lighten up' by being less serious and rule bound in their approach. If they avoided being too long-winded in explaining or blaming others, they would irritate others far less. They should try to be less sensitive to criticism. Not everyone is focused on facts alone, and awareness of the Withdrawns' emotions will create more empathy to resolve conflict.

Dealing with conflict as a Withdrawn Type –
Typically includes Enneagram Types Four, Five and Nine.

Withdrawns are firm about how others should be aware of their emotions and how emotionally vulnerable they can be when faced with conflict. They are clear regarding their need to be treated with sensitivity, warning others that they are likely to take things personally. An expectation that others should read their moods and body language is expressed. They are able to articulate how their family and childhood experiences have influenced their way of dealing with conflict.

They express a need to be given time out to gather themselves and to deal with their own thoughts and emotions before being confronted by others. Unless there is some level of trust, they are not willing to engage with others. Any sign of 'attack' by others will cause to them to withdraw entirely from conflict.

They are reactive regarding how others should treat them in situations of conflict by expecting others to 'wake them up'; 'come and find us'; and 'give us guidelines on dealing with difficult situations'. There is a clear expectation that others should take the initiative to engage them when they have withdrawn. They request others to tap into their creativity and ideas as a way of resolving conflict. They are even more definite than the Compliant group about their need to be dealt with in private.

Humour is encouraged as a way to defuse the emotional discomfort of conflict. There is a note of irony in their expressing that they have more difficulty in dealing with the Assertive group during conflict than with the Compliant group. The Withdrawn group demonstrates the need to withdraw from others in order to capture their emotional balance. It is pertinent that they also warn others that their withdrawing should not be interpreted as their belief that they have lost the argument.

Advice for Withdrawns

Withdrawns should attempt to be less sensitive and be more willing to state their viewpoint directly. They should also state their needs without apology and not expect others to read their minds. They should not shrink away from their more Assertive or Compliant colleagues, friends of family. Being moody or sulking about an issue does not resolve subliminal conflict. They should take responsibility for their own behaviour and not expect others to pick up on their emotions. They should initiate difficult discussions and not always wait for others to take the lead.

Making peace with conflict

It is not suggested that we aspire to a tensionless state, devoid of paradoxes and conflict, as this is not conducive to a soulful life, since we gain vitality from tension, we learn from paradoxes, and we gain wisdom and self-confidence by coping with the contradictory, confusing and complex multiplicity of the soul. The sign of a soulful life is its rich texture and its complexity. The soul complexes, therefore, are not to be simply ironed out, because they are the stuff of human complexity.

In the following chapter we will explore how knowledge of our Enneagram type can bring us more clarity and peace in life.

CHAPTER FIFTEEN

Tribal satisfaction –

Waking up to our true selves

WITH DEEPER KNOWLEDGE OF SELF and others comes clarity and forgiveness. we are truly able to understand firstly our own and then others' way of seeing e world, we can stop finding fault with others and then setting out to try to ange people. It is known that no matter how much goodwill there is, we cannot rsuade the alcoholic to stop drinking, the overweight to go on diet, or another return our affections unless they have the free will to choose their actions.

It is wonderful how people do start responding positively to us when we just mpletely accept them for whom they are. This is called unconditional love, and nen we think about it, it is sheer arrogance to place any conditions on others to her like or love us when we ourselves are so blinded by our own nonsense.

Ouspensky (2001), a pupil of Gurdjieff who brought the Enneagram to the est, distinguished two types of psychology: the study of man as he is and e study of man as he can become. When individuals have ascertained what nneagram type they are, they can do one of two things: let it be or use this owledge for self-improvement.

Access to the Enneagram model is freely available as it has not been licensed patented by any entity or individual. As a human resource practitioner and t a psychologist, my field of interest always lay in finding a model that would ve practical application in enabling employees to have clarity in viewing their haviour through an 'unblemished lens'. The observations which I have gained normal daily interactions with others, and more specifically through coaching ple, have validated the accuracy of the Enneagram model. Coachees were e to view their behaviour and identify with their habitual ways of being in derstanding their Enneagram type. These were conclusions reached by the chees and not by me in my role as the coach.

It is in this way that the Enneagram is a powerful tool to be held as a mirror others to observe their own behaviour and then to make choices about wing up in a more effective way. The Enneagram is also not simply a set ine boxes, or categories, to classify individuals and then make sweeping

observations about their collective behaviour. It has been illustrated tha
the complexities and permutations in the wings, the subtypes, the Centre
the levels of development and the points of integration and disintegratio
do not allow for this. These dimensions create a different nuance to ever
type, and result in people behaving differently even if they are of the sam
basic type.

Belief systems, personal values, nurturing, culture and education also hav
an influence on how people behave. However, many people find themselv
stuck in 'boxes of malcontent' – of confusion, conflict and unhappiness – an
the Enneagram can be the ladder to guide them out.

When people accept that they are born with an inherent personality typ
they tend to be more forgiving of their own and others' blind spots. They a
also less likely to blame their parents, teachers and childhood experience
and are likely to be more willing to take responsibility for their own se
development and EQ growth. I do not suggest that Enneagram type is the on
factor influencing people in how they behave, but it is an important aspect
personality motivations.

Knowledge of the Enneagram also frees people from believing that their l
stories define who they are. They are able to let go of the narratives that impris
them and instead can embrace constructivism in choosing to change throug
different meaning ascribed to their life circumstances and relationships.

It is important to note, however, that personal motivation and choices are mc
useful than a simple knowledge of the Enneagram typology and behavioural tra
but awareness of people's automatic responses and the emotional 'froth' that c
cloud their judgement can be a powerful tool in understanding behaviour. W
this awareness, people can widen their choices of behaviour to engage mc
effectively in the workplace, with friends and with their families.

Some people persist in using 'their pictures of the world' even when the
repeatedly and consistently let them down. For example, when someo
persists in classifying others as hostile even though they actually want to h
that person. There is inadequate contact with reality: often we forget that o
first impressions do not provide us with sound predictions.

A general characteristic of disturbed people is that they believe that th
problems are caused by the circumstances of their lives, whereas in rea
their problems derive from their interpretation of those circumstances. I
that people need never be victims of their own biographies.

People usually do the best that they can with the knowledge or intellige

nat they have at the time of their actions. We can only become happy adults
rhen we are able to forgive our parents for their perceived follies, and this only
appens when we are able to truly understand them. In living our present lives
s parents we have the potential to meet our responsibility in gaining the highest
ossible EQ to ensure that we can appear as functional parents and in turn
uide our children to develop optimum understanding of their behaviour.

It is in this way that the Enneagram has been immensely liberating for some
dividuals. They are able to separate themselves from the repeated stories of
eir childhood experiences and other histories. They also understand that,
wing to their personality type, they may be predisposed to behave in certain
ays. Their personal development lies in the awareness that they are able to
oose different ways of reacting to situations.

There may be times when the relationships we find ourselves in are
sfunctional and cause us great unhappiness. If we have really shown our
st intentions in responding with love and understanding and the other being
ll makes us unhappy and is turning us into a human pretzel, then I advocate
ving the courage to terminate the relationship. Too many times people remain
relationships due to guilt, fear and misplaced compassion. This applies to
ployment relationships, friendships, marriages and families.

It is amazing, when we do end these toxic relationships, how often we make
om for new and uplifting experiences with others. It is as if we clear the
bwebs and allow our constructive energies to be channelled to those who
serve our love and energy. I am not advocating the practice of easy divorce,
pecially if motivated by one partner's temporary lust for another which leaves
rail of destruction, most especially if there are children involved. We should
very clear that before severing a relationship that it is not because of our own
k of insight into our own blind spots that could be causing the conflict. It
ps to check this out with a trusted mentor, coach, friend or therapist.

e stages of change

s important that it is understood what happens when individuals attempt to
ange. Prochaska and Clemente (1997) define a model of behaviour change
ntified in six stages:

Pre-contemplation
Here individuals are engaged in behaviour that they wish to change.
mplicit in the wish is a lack of intent to change behaviour.

- **Contemplation**
  At this stage individuals start to consider the possibility of changing. However, they also see the advantages of staying as they are.
- **Preparation**
  Here individuals take steps to change their behaviour. They make minor adjustments to their thought patterns. Often individuals who ask for coaching have reached this stage.
- **Action**
  Here individuals are actively engaged in the new behaviour. They have found their target and identified ways of meeting it. They may also be searching for ways of overcoming any problems that might stop them from maintaining the new behaviour.
- **Maintenance**
  At this stage individuals sustain behavioural change over time. They work to prevent relapse and to reinforce the gains of the action stage.
- **Termination**
  This stage is marked by a perceptible lack of temptation to behave in the old ways.

You, dear reader, need to identify what it is you wish to change, why it is necessary to change, what the benefits will be to you and others to make this change – and decide where you are in the six steps outlined above.

Respectful use of the Enneagram

People who use the model should also be mindful about using the Enneagram in an ethical manner. This has reference to the following points:

- Enneagram students should be actively discouraged from attempting to typecast others in a labelling kind of way. Not only are these attempts often inaccurate, but they can also be perceived as intrusive to others, because they tend to make people feel that someone is making judgements about behaviour that they do not own. Behaviour traits may be easy to observe, but only the individual understands the motivation for the behaviour.
- Similarly, Enneagram teachers should also desist from attempting to typecast their students. Even if they have excellent knowledge of the system, they do not have divine insight into others' motives for behaviour. Sometimes people need guidance in understanding these motives. Teachers and coaches should encourage this exploration by asking coaching

questions rather than imposing their opinions on their students. This process of enquiry creates a climate where the most self-reflection and the greatest learning occur.

It is again stressed at all times that no one type is better than another and all types are needed in every business and social sphere. People should rather be invited to reflect on where they may find themselves regarding their level of development (or emotional intelligence) and how they are affected by stress or conflict situations.

Practising self-awakening

In my experience this is different for each of us. Not everyone 'finds themselves' through meditation and I do not believe that it is in any way helpful to beat ourselves up when we cannot follow a practice which might be punted as the nirvana for the human race.

Of course it is wonderful if people are able to find peace and personal growth through meditation or prayer, but as has been illustrated in the chapters for the different Enneagram types, we are unlikely to follow the same paths to peace and better productivity in life.

Some coaches recommend different methods for specific types, but I have found that the best way is for us to experiment with all that is out there and then focus on what really works for us as individuals. I also recommend that you be taught properly to practise, rather than just trying and giving up before you have learned the proper techniques. I attended a course in meditation which I found very helpful in 'getting it'.

It is still my personal preference to walk alone with my pug dog on the beach and to absorb the changing colours and shapes of the mountains around us in Hout Bay and to allow the solitude, thoughts of gratitude and hope to fill my soul until the next walk.

In this way, dear reader, you may find that keeping a journal, riding your bike, doing yoga, colouring in, jogging, a dream journal, painting, pottery, massage, listening to or performing music, hiking, poetry, gardening, surfing, finger painting, Rolfing, charity work, mentorship, swimming … and so I can continue … is the activity or combination that takes you to that deep and true place within yourself when you experience the wonder and joy of being a human being. What matters is that we find the time to do these wholesome activities which remove us from just being on automatic drive.

We also need to be conscious of how we are 'paying forward'. This is not about doing acts of kindness which we advertise or for which we seek some recognition. It is rather in the true sense of *ubuntu* that we are actively committed to giving of our time or resources to a person, community or cause where we can make even a small difference. The act of giving brings all the gratification and spiritual reward which ultimately makes life a richer experience.

A practice which leads to emotional health is one that lifts us out of the weary existence and allows us to observe ourselves as sentient and wondrous creatures who are willing and able to live our lives to the fullest.

Enjoying a more balanced lifestyle can be informed with more awareness of the Centres. This relates to our being aware of the clarity of our thoughts, our emotional climate and how we choose to take action or non-action when we are stimulated by any situation in life.

Human beings are mysterious

The paradox I have discovered in studying the Enneagram is that the more I believe I understand human behaviour, the more mystery I find in people. The Enneagram cannot predict behaviour and we should not choose to use it in this way. It is naïve to think that 'now I have your number, I have some power over you'. This kind of misplaced logic will only bring about suffering and disappointment.

I find that the more accepting I am towards others and enjoy their moments of surprise, the more they show me the lighter side of themselves. When I am disappointed in another I need to reflect whether in fact I am projecting my own blind spots and whether the disappointment I am experiencing is not my 'own chickens coming home to roost'. The example for my type is experiencing deceit. When as a Type Three I feel distrustful of others, I may well be projecting deceit in the false belief that I may be imagining the deceit without any foundation of this being so. A practical example of this is that I might tell 'white lies' from time to time, and then falsely accuse one of my children of telling a lie.

In the same way Type Eights can experience others as being confrontational, Type Ones see others as being unnecessarily critical, Type Twos believe others are selfish, Type Fours may think others envy them, Type Fives think others are withholding from them, Type Sixes experience others as paranoid and Type Sevens might believe people are greedy. We can learn so much about our own fixations in carefully reflecting on what we act out towards others.

way to realising our true potential

is by using and developing our creative soul gifts that we can be fully
npowered to jointly create a more wholesome world. For this to become a
ew way of being, we need to awaken from the nightmare of seeing ourselves
 limited beings. The more we hold to a diminished image of humanity, the
 ore we become swallowed by low self-esteem, hopelessness and fear. When we
 lieve ourselves to be without talent and power, we lack the energy we need to
 ing in new visions of wholeness and connection with all life. Instead, we act as
 ctims and accept the dictates of a few who feed us images of destruction and
 oject to us a sense of hopelessness (Cornell 2002).

I have always been aware of the advantage and disadvantage of embarking on
 riting about a subject that I unequivocally love. I have, however, attempted to
 ustrate the theory in demonstrating the robust and pragmatic properties of
 e Enneagram as a compass to guide people as they embark on the journey of
coming more self-aware. The more I work with people the more I realise how
 ly mysterious we are. This is so because we have the capacity to disappoint
 d to delight. It is therefore essential that we treat the Enneagram lightly and
 t become evangelical with its distinctions. I remain eternally in love with the
 neagram for the lightness it has brought to me and all those with whom I
joy connection.

Once we have recognised our Enneagram type or tribe, and learned more
 out how we can grow and what we can choose to avoid, we can start
 covering how each of the types can bring us guidance to show up as truly
 egrated beings.

Within each of us is a ray of light flowing from the depth of our being. When
 s light penetrates our consciousness, we stand in that perfect moment on the
 e path of our life. This true path is what we are all looking for – in everything
 do and everything we pursue. We must start on a real pilgrimage, a long
 grimage. We are near enough now to look one another straight in the eyes,
 ching beyond the eyes, into the depths of living hearts. It is all too easy to
 in the other what repels us and makes strangers of them, and to see in those
 o are on our side nothing but the most attractive qualities (Rabbin 2004).

My invitation to you, dear reader, is to use the knowledge of the Enneagram
 getting to know yourself better and treating yourself and all other people to
 om you relate with more kindness, forgiveness and appreciation.

RECOMMENDED READING FOR FURTHER EXPLORATION OF THE ENNEAGRAM

Almaas, A.H. (2006) *Brilliancy: The Essence of Intelligence.* London: Shambhala.

Baron, R. & Wagele, E. (1994) *The Enneagram Made Easy.* New York: Harper Collins.

Bast, M. & Clarence, T. (2006) *Out of the Box: Coaching Field Guide.* Louisbur KS: Ninestar Publishing.

Horsley, M. (2005) *The Enneagram for the Spirit.* London: Gaia Books.

Lapid-Bogda, G. (2004) *Bringing out the Best in Yourself at Work: How to Use t Enneagram System for Success.* New York: McGraw-Hill Books.

Maitri, S. (2005) *The Enneagram of Passions and Virtues: Finding the Way Hom* New York: Penguin.

Nathans, H. (2004) *The Enneagram at Work.* London: Cyan Scriptum.

Palmer, H. (1988) *Understanding Yourself and the Others in Your Life.* New Yor Harper Collins.

Palmer, H. (1995) *The Enneagram in Love and Work: Understanding your Busin and Intimate Relationships.* New York: Harper Collins.

Riso, D.R. (1993) *Enneagram Transformations.* New York: Houghton Mifflin.

Riso, D.R. & Hudson, R. (1996) *Personality Types.* New York: Hought Mifflin.

Riso, D.R. & Hudson, R. (1999) *The Wisdom of the Enneagram.* New Yo Houghton Mifflin.

Riso, D.R. & Hudson, R. (2000) *Understanding the Enneagram.* New Yo Houghton Mifflin.

Riso, D.R. & Hudson, R. (2003) *Discovering your Personality Type.* New Yo Houghton Mifflin Company.

Sikora, M. & Tallon, R. (2006) *Awareness to Action.* Scranton: University Scranton Press.

REFERENCES

Cornell, S. (2002) *The Soul of Creativity*. London: Routledge.

Coleman, D. (1999) *Working with Emotional Intelligence*. London: Bloomsbury Publishing.

Kraepelin, E. Diagnostics and Statistical Manual of Mental Disorders. http://www.psych.org

Kraepelin, E. (1913) *Psychiatry* (8th ed.) Leipzig: J.A. Barth.

Maturana, H.R. (2004) *From Being to Doing: The Origins of the Biology of Cognition*. Carl Auer Verlag.

Nevid, J.S., Rathus, S.A. & Greene, B. (2003) *Abnormal Psychology in a Changing World* (5th ed.) New Jersey : Prentice Hall.

Ouspensky, P.D. (2001) *In Search of the Miraculous*. USA: Harvest Books.

Nicoll, M. (1985) *Psychological Commentaries on the Teachings of Gurdjieff and Ouspensky*. London: Shambhala.

Palmer, H. (1988) *Understanding the Enneagram*. New York: Harper Collins.

Prochaska, J.O. & Clemente, C.C. (1997) The trans-theoretical model of behaviour change. *American Journal of Health*, 12: 38–48.

Robbin, R. (2004) Finding our way. http://www.workasplay.com

Riso, D.R. & Hudson, R. (1996) *Personality Types*. New York : Houghton Mifflin.

Riso, D.R. & Hudson, R. (1999) *The Wisdom of the Enneagram*. New York: Houghton Mifflin.

Riso, D.R. & Hudson, R. Training Workshops http://www.ennegraminstitute.com

Sikora, M. (2006) The subtypes at work. http://www.mariosikora.com

Sikora, M. & Tallon, R. (2006) *Awareness to Action*. Chicago: University of Scranton Press.